'This book demonstrates that S. Freud's adolescent crisis is far from being calm, despite the appearance that he gave of it. It is certainly upsetting, rich in emotions, creative, questioning. Was adolescence so disliked because it was at the very origin of Freudian thought? To what extent did Freud try all his life to find his buried adolescence? In the same way, an adolescence refused in its difficulty could, in its time, become a privileged source of metapsychology and its technical corollaries. The richness of the "biographic-theoretical" field opened by Florian Houssier's book is thus an event.'

Philippe Gutton, *Psychiatrist, Psychoanalyst, University Professor,*
Founder of the Revue Adolescence (France)

This book was translated by Kristina Valendinova, psychotherapist and psycho-analyst in London.

The translation of this book was financially supported by the Transversal Research Unit: Psychogenesis and Psychopathology (UTRPP – UR 4403), University of Paris 13, Villetaneuse, Sorbonne Paris Nord (SPN) – France.

Freud's Adolescence

In *Freud's Adolescence*, Florian Houssier looks at the early years of the Father of Psychoanalysis and considers how his personal experiences shaped his later work. Including excerpts from many letters written by Freud himself, this volume allows a rare glimpse into the inner thoughts and emotions of one of his generation's greatest minds.

Engaging with this lesser-known period of Freud's life, the vivacity of his incestuous and parricidal fantasies comes to the surface, infiltrating his relational life as well as his dreams. Houssier proposes a new hypothesis about the conflicts of Freud's adolescence, and their impact on his tendencies in later conflicts. This is the first book that sustains a systematic analysis of this material and adds a new dimension to the biography of Freud by exploring links between his life and creativity from a current theorisation of the adolescent process.

This book will be an essential read for all psychoanalysts, psychologists, lecturers, followers of Freud's work and those looking into psychoanalysis as a whole.

Florian Houssier is a clinical psychologist and psychoanalyst (Société de Psychanalyse Freudienne). He is Professor of Clinical Psychology and Psychopathology at the Sorbonne, France; Director of the Laboratory Transversal Unit of Research: Psychogenesis and Psychopathology (UTRPP – UR 4403); and President of the Collège International de L'Adolescence (CILA).

Freud's Adolescence

Oedipus Complex and Parricidal Tendencies

Florian Houssier

Routledge
Taylor & Francis Group

LONDON AND NEW YORK

Designed cover image: GeorgiosArt / Getty Images

First published in English 2023
by Routledge
4 Park Square, Milton Park, Abingdon, Oxon OX14 4RN

and by Routledge
605 Third Avenue, New York, NY 10158

Routledge is an imprint of the Taylor & Francis Group, an informa business

Published in French by Campagne-Première/SPF-CP/First Campaign editions 2018

British Library Cataloguing-in-Publication Data
A catalogue record for this book is available from the British Library

Library of Congress Cataloging-in-Publication Data
Names: Houssier, Florian, author.
Title: Freud's adolescence : Oedipus complex and parricidal tendencies / Florian Houssier.
Description: 1 Edition. | New York, NY : Routledge, 2023. | Includes bibliographical references and index.
Identifiers: LCCN 2022037703 (print) | LCCN 2022037704 (ebook) | ISBN 9781032375748 (paperback) | ISBN 9781032375755 (hardback) | ISBN 9781003340898 (ebook)
Subjects: LCSH: Freud, Sigmund, 1856–1939. | Psychoanalysis. | Adolescent analysis. | Oedipus complex. | Psychoanalysts—Austria—Biography.
Classification: LCC BF109.F74 H684 2023 (print) | LCC BF109.F74 (ebook) | DDC 150.19/52—dc23/eng/20221017
LC record available at https://lccn.loc.gov/2022037703
LC ebook record available at https://lccn.loc.gov/2022037704

ISBN: 978-1-032-37575-5 (hbk)
ISBN: 978-1-032-37574-8 (pbk)
ISBN: 978-1-003-34089-8 (ebk)

DOI: 10.4324/9781003340898

Typeset in Times New Roman
by Apex CoVantage, LLC

Contents

Chapter 1

Introduction

As it will often be the case in this book, let's begin by quoting Freud himself, when, looking back over his life's journey, he writes: "Two themes run through these pages: the story of my life and the history of psycho-analysis. They are intimately interwoven" (1925, p. 70). This is the path we will follow: starting from his biography and looking for the ways in which his adolescence was reflected in his later theory. This is a method Freud himself employed regularly, using biographical fragments to support his discoveries and theoretical hypotheses. As Jean-Baptiste Pontalis writes, "Whether they like it or not, psychoanalysts are also subject to the effects of history, not just those of their family stories" (Pontalis, 1976, p. 4).

1.1 Adolescent psychoanalysis: the French perspective

The theoretical richness of the French field of adolescent psychoanalysis seems unparalleled. Starting from the present moment, this book wishes to trace the genealogical origins of these theories, from Freud to current authors. In a previous work, I followed a similar genealogical link between Freud and his daughter Anna, examining the back-and-forth movement between father and daughter on both biographical and theoretical levels (Houssier, 2011b). Adding to this "theoretical reciprocity" between the two generations, I will also look at Winnicott, whose theoretical proximity to Anna Freud's ideas on adolescence has already been shown (Houssier and Vlachopoulou, 2015). The further developments of Winnicott's thought, as illustrated by the brilliant work of Rene Roussillon, are linked to this original kinship, and I will be careful not to separate Anna Freud's ideas on adolescence from those of her father.

The "Big Bang" of adolescent psychoanalysis in France happened in the early 1980s. Following the work of Pierre Mâle and Evelyne Kestemberg, a new generation of psychoanalysts kicked the proverbial hornet's nest. This included the essential work of Philippe Gutton (2004), who created, in 1983, the first and only psychoanalytically oriented scientific journal dedicated to the questions of adolescence, disrupting, at the time not without a certain degree of controversy, the

DOI: 10.4324/9781003340898-1

neat binary between infantile psychic life and adult psychopathology. As part of the same movement and two years after having founded the journal *Adolescence*, Gutton created the first university research team working on this topic, the Adolescence Research Unit at the University of Paris Diderot. In 1995, this research unit gave rise to the idea of the International College of Adolescence (Collège International de l'Adolescence, CILA) directed by the psychoanalyst and scholar Annie Birraux. This initial impetus – founding a journal and a university laboratory which began to produce a large number of doctoral theses on questions of adolescence – coincided with a growing interest among lacanian psychoanalysts, starting with the work of Jean-Jacques Rassial, and helped constitute an extremely rich theoretical movement which, over the past thirty years in France, has shown few signs of losing steam, as evidenced by the continuing stream of publications and the importance adolescent psychoanalysis now enjoys among French psychoanalytic groups.

These preliminary reflections, though far from exhaustive, might give an impression of a certain culture-centrism. In my personal case, this is nonetheless based on having attended numerous conferences abroad, especially those organised by the CILA, which over time strengthened my hypothesis. It remains to be seen whether this idea is useful and, if so, why has French psychoanalysis been on the leading edge of this field. Perhaps it has to do with the fact that despite having been subject to numerous attacks, psychoanalysis has maintained its position in France, and with a political and cultural context that was particularly favourable to this exploration. However, to this day, there has been no attempt in France to go beyond these theoretical and clinical genealogies and examine what has so far been the poor relative of the many biographies dedicated to Freud; this evokes an image used by Anna Freud, who called adolescence "the Cinderella of psychoanalysis" (Freud, 1958).

Before we start, let me express two wishes concerning the history of psychoanalysis. First, that the day when the linguistic barriers fall, we will be able to bring together the different ideas of all those rare psychoanalysts interested in the history of their discipline and overcome our ignorance. This ignorance – and this is not an exaggeration – is maintained at the risk of a repetition compulsion at work in both academic teaching and inside psychoanalytic institutions, a tireless rehashing of inexact or ideologically biased ideas. This insular transmission of an adversarial and therefore limited debate goes far beyond the walls of particular institutions; the absence of doctoral dissertations by psychoanalysts or of a scientific journal dedicated to the history of psychoanalysis shows that there is still a long way to go in France, despite the importance of the work of Elisabeth Roudinesco and Alain de Mijolla. And yet, exploring the history of psychoanalysis is one way of expanding its theory, boosting its dynamism and preventing its calcification.

Immersing ourselves in history by carefully recontextualising the framework of propositions and hypotheses mobilised by the material discovered is not a process aimed at formulating a truth, which is always relative and plural. Historical research, the close cousin of psychoanalytic practice, works across three dimensions: clinical, theoretical and biographical.

By exploring the intricacies of Freud's biography, we (re)discover the archaeological passion for excavation by weaving a thread of associations between these three areas. As a result, we get a glimpse of a historical era and its social codes. Freud as a man of his time cannot be separated from his theory without the risk of splitting or fetishising his ideas. Looking at his conflicts as a young man paints a different portrait, a different image of a complex human being, against the kaleidoscope of representations gathered over the past hundred years. Contrary to caricatural simplifications, historical research espouses complexity, reducing the tendency to idolise the founder of psychoanalysis. During his life, Freud already produced several historical texts, both on the history of the psychoanalytic movement and his own theoretical journey; however, to the chagrin of his future biographers, he also destroyed some of his letters. What can we say about the traces left by him? His wish to remain discreet about his private life appears to contradict what I have discovered while writing this book, namely that his texts are full of extracts from his own life, his memories of childhood and boyhood. In the light of this material, theory is no longer a self-generated work but, at least partially, biographically created; this is an important difference.

1.2 Travelling in Freudland

What are the risks of such a journey into Freudland? Is Freud not there to defend himself? This investigation should not be seen as a game of attack and defence, but rather of settling a debt to Freud, in line with the potentially transgressive fantasies of trying to understand the sharp edges of adolescent conflict or clearing the way into what is still largely a *terra incognita*. Can Freud as a subject be analysed? Can we use the tools of applied analysis to turn him into a kind of clinical case? The question remains open, but we can at least say that despite his love of letter burning – a teenage gesture par excellence – Freud left behind a considerable amount of autobiographical material contained in the letters received and preserved by his correspondents.

Without systematically following the chronology of these letters but instead combining them into thematic tracks, I will look at Freud's correspondence to identify the lines of tension, the beating of a pulse. Among the few fantasies I will allow myself, I will follow the movements of young Freud's heart, alternating between the names of those he was closest to, namely his friend Eduard Silberstein and later his fiancée Martha Bernays. Such resorting to given names is a form of familiarity, where characters become well-known persons with imaginable feelings. This relationship to Freud's loved ones betrays both a movement of identification and a form of transference, not just to Freud but also to his world.

These movements of transference are part of the work of researching the history of psychoanalysis, between the necessary distance and the proximity required to enter the author's subjective space. Often have I chosen to let Freud speak for himself, at the risk of adhering too closely to his manifest discourse; I have taken this position for a number of different reasons. Giving the floor back to Freud is a way of allowing the reader to make his own opinion. Too many misconceptions arise from not having the potential of a more pluralistic analysis. Letting Freud speak is also a way of grasping and analysing the abundance of the material on his teenage years, which has so far remained underused despite its obvious fruitfulness. This raises the question of why this essential period of Freud's life has been relatively forgotten and provokes new hypotheses about the status of adolescence in his life and work. Finally, returning to Freud's speech gives homage to his prose, full of dazzling fulgurations to which no synthesis can fully do justice. The recurrent terms or expressions open up significant interpretative avenues to understanding Freud's own youth and exploring his literary and mythological references. It is therefore by his side and in listening to him that I will try to make my arguments, following the associative method. The image of a journey has a special place among the fantasies present in the writing of this book; it evokes Freud's process when visiting Greece and the Acropolis in 1904, accompanied by his brother Alexander. As he explained thirty-two years later to Romain Rolland, the view from the Acropolis provoked a certain disturbance in him, a sense of the uncanny, when, in discovering these faraway lands and famous landscapes, he exceeded the accomplishments of his own father (Freud, 1936). Once again, in this now classic text the elements of Freud's biography and his theoretical work come close enough to merge into a single whole. Freud took the central route in the social sciences, by adopting the subjectivity of the therapist/researcher and turning the object studied into a chemical mixture of regular back-and-forth movements, of insights and blind spots, of more or less elaborated personal conflicts, only to eventually conclude that although it did not hinder the discovery of ideas, this subjectivity ultimately served the creative process. His analysis of clinical cases also demonstrated the universal nature of individual conflicts.

Writing about Freud as a man and a psychoanalyst necessarily involves moments of identification. This is one of the key elements of the transference to the father of psychoanalysis, probably tinged with a touch of adolescence that continues to live on within us and that mobilises a certain defiance, a hint of provocation, not to mention certain fantasies of omnipotence – a form of familiarity oscillating between identifying with Freud's genius and calling him into question.

However, the aim is not an inflammatory critique, such as that presented by a so-called philosopher keen to announce the twilight of psychoanalysis. This kind of putting psychoanalysis on trial tends to rely on material that is perfectly familiar to its historians but is presented as new and definitive. And though there is indeed nothing new about this type of intellectual charlatanism, one that continuously takes things out of context, it does have effects on the less well-informed public; hence the importance of systematically refreshing the biographical work that humanises Freud without constantly searching for supposedly shocking revelations. One of the challenges of this project is to stay away from any kind of value judgment on Freud, maintaining a strictly scientific approach, not forgetting that Freud was also someone who, both in his life and in his work, repeatedly presented a certain ethics of truth, no matter how painful.

The serious work of the historians of psychoanalysis has identified a number of core issues relevant to this undertaking. First, reading some of the major biographies of Freud shows that his adolescence is the least researched period of his life (Rodrigué, 2000) and thus, so far, the least thought about. It is the subject of only a handful of articles, which by the way are very interesting, and the few books that actually discuss it never do so based on a theory of adolescence as a process.

Ultimately, there are three documents that give us a more precise idea of what Freud's adolescence was like. First, his work on dream analysis, which is full of memories of his youth. Second, two other sources have been key: the letters of his youth, especially to his best friend at the time, Eduard Silberstein (Freud, 1871–1881). Prior to their publication in 1989, authors such as Klumpner (1978) believed that there was no link between Freud's own adolescent development and his theorisation of it, which we find especially in the third *Essay on the Theory of Sexuality* (Freud, 1905a); he says it would be strange to think otherwise. The author adds that prior to 1905 Freud had treated at least twelve adolescent patients, with varying success, using a kind of psycho-pedagogical dialogue on sexuality. These young people were aged between eleven and twenty; the author also mentions a dozen more potential cases which are less certain. The method of treatment varied, from psychoanalysis to hypnotic catharsis, and included persuasion, daily visits in a sanatorium or the establishment of a diagnosis; they were generally of short duration. This book wants to make a decidedly opposite argument and demonstrate the importance of these letters to Freud's understanding of adolescence. Clinically, I was also able to establish the sinuous yet close connection between the discovery of psychoanalysis and the proliferation of the cases of adolescent patients in Freud's practice (Houssier and Christaki, 2016).

1.3 Generational transmission

From a biographical perspective, there are two main views on Freud's adolescence. An article by Alain De Mijolla (1996) explored this topic to conclude that it was a fairly tranquil period, which nevertheless then had an effect, as a form of deferred action, on his forties (De Mijolla, 2003). We shall see that a more detailed examination of Freud's adolescence reveals a number of psychic wounds and great degree of mental distress. At the same time, I agree with the second argument: the idea of a deferred return to adolescence is very important, also because the concept of deferred action was key in the creation of psychoanalysis (Houssier and Christaki, 2016).

Eissler (1978), whose perspective I share, disagrees with, for example, Jones' (1958) or Gedo and Wolf's versions (1970), which also see Freud's adolescence as uncomplicated. I believe it is no coincidence that their analysis not just differs from but contrasts with that of Eissler, who in fact specialised in adolescence and its disorders (Marty, 2002). For the psychoanalyst trying his hand at writing, the relationship to debt concerns not just one's transference to Freud but necessarily follows in the footsteps of Freud's first post-mortem biographer, Siegfried Bernfeld, the author of a pioneering work on adolescent psychoanalysis. However, the key point is this: without a true grasp of the process of adolescence and its traumatic potential, we risk missing out on the vibrancy of its conflicts and challenges. Also, and surprisingly, Freud's main biographers make almost no use of the idea of adolescence as revelatory of the infantile to understand the subtleties of Freud's psychic conflicts.

Autobiographical sources coming from Freud himself suggest that adolescence was both a source of nostalgia (it was the good time) and sexual longing (not missing the right opportunity, having his pick among several women and enjoying more sexual freedom), but also of failure, humiliation, inhibition, poverty, in other words, no doubt the most painful period of his life. A generation later, a connection appeared clearly in his preoccupation with whether he would live long enough to support his children and especially his sons during their adolescence, and thus his implicit fear of not surviving, as a father, his sons' pubertal growth. We could also mention the effect of transmission, both personal and theoretical-clinical, between himself and his daughter Anna, who was an unwanted child and was then expected to be a son named Wilhelm (after Fliess). Which, in a sense, is who she became: a tomboy, her father's intellectual companion, his narcissistic double and a source of transmission of the cause, psychoanalysis being the theoretical offspring shared and cared for by them as a couple.

She was also named after the daughter of young Freud's professor of religion, Samuel Hammerschlag, to whom he dedicated a brilliant homage in an obituary published in *Die Neue Frei Presse* (Freud, 1904).

Later, as the custodian of unresolved adolescent conflicts, Anna spearheaded the pioneering investigation of the adolescent process (Houssier, 2010a), following the path paved by her father. Her particular emphasis on the defensive aspects of adolescence should therefore not surprise us; adolescence as a defensive crisis involves both intellectualisation and asceticism, which concerned both father and daughter, suggesting that Anna's work on adolescence cannot be understood without a reference to her father's positions, but also that some of her own internal conflicts speak to what her father himself had not been able to resolve.

1.4 A pivotal period: 1895–1905

Since *Studies on Hysteria* (Freud and Breuer, 1895), Freud regularly made a link between adolescence and understanding hysteria, a connection supported by the discovery of the concept of deferred action (Freud, 1895a). Unless we are dealing directly with young people, memories of adolescence only come to the surface retroactively. For example, in the case of Cěcilie M., adolescence appears as a source of her psychogenic disorder (Freud, 1900, p. 521):

> As long ago as in 1895 I was able to give an explanation (. . .) of the first hysterical attack which a woman of over forty had had in her fifteenth year.

The Interpretation of Dreams is full of material on adolescence. The period of writing this work, which remained one of Freud's favourites alongside *Totem and Taboo* (1913), seems central to the elaboration of his own adolescence, in a retroactive biographical and theoretical movement and through his self-analysis. We have also shown (Houssier and Christaki, 2016) that the text was greatly influenced by Freud's clinical work with young patients, in which he was deeply involved. At a crossroads between his so-called hypnosis period (Freud and Breuer, 1895) and the birth of psychoanalysis, the book emerged against the backdrop of Freud's correspondence with Fliess (Freud, 1986), a relationship which replaced his previous passionate friendship with Silberstein (Houssier, 2013b).

While finishing the dream book, in late 1899, Freud also met one of his most famous patients, Dora. In a similar perspective, bringing together dream analysis, adolescence and clinical cases, Freud initially thought of the Dora case as a follow-up on *The Interpretation of Dreams*, written to illustrate and support his hypotheses on hysteria announced as early as in 1895. The original title of the case study was "Dreams and Hysteria". During the treatment, which lasted less than three months and was broken off by Dora on 31st December 1899, he continued to study dreams by focusing on two dreams of his young female patient (Freud, 1905b).

Let's return to the role Freud gives to puberty. At the time, the term "adolescence" was not commonly used in German, contrary to *Pubertät*, which means that we have to clarify whether Freud is speaking about a physiological event or, as it is more often the case, adolescence more generally. The Fliess correspondence belongs to the particular period of Freud's key discoveries, which were subsequently elaborated further. It was also during this time of intensive self-analysis that he made links between his own memories of childhood and at times puberty and what his patients would relate to him.

> My work with neurotic patients has taught me the nature of the memories of which this is a favourite method of representation. They are occasions on which the subject has turned over the pages of encyclopaedias or dictionaries in order (like most people at the inquisitive age of puberty) to satisfy their craving for an answer to the riddles of sex.
>
> (Freud, 1900, p. 530, n1)

This hunger for sexual knowledge is not something that only appears in adolescence; however, it initiates a retroactive movement that is not simply a repetition of the infantile sexual investigations but uses new mental and emotional resources to satisfy this curiosity by one's own means, the subjectivation linked to the process of adolescence.

In his practice as well as the theoretical work derived from it, Freud highlighted the shocking nature of sexual "matters" and their impact on the imagination of chaste young girls. Hence, he associated the hysterical dimension with a loss of the purity of feelings. He writes:

> With children of ten, of twelve, or of fourteen, with boys and girls alike, I have satisfied myself that the truth of this statement can invariably be relied upon.
>
> (Freud, 1905b, p. 48)

Later in the text, this does not prevent him from discussing the Oedipus complex of future neurotics by invoking the affective hunger of precocious children or the excitement produced by spontaneous genital sensations, a scene of seduction or masturbation. He argues that in such cases, certain other influences come into play to create a fixation of the ordinary feeling of love so that

> it turns into something (either while the child is still young or *not until it has reached the age of puberty*) which must be put on a par with a sexual inclination and which, like the latter, has the forces of the libido at its command.
>
> (Ibid., p. 55–56, my emphasis)

The essential thread running through this decade includes the discovery of the points of contact between adolescence and the infantile or of hysterical conflicts, based on Freud's clinical work with young people or with older patients describing the often-traumatic episodes of their youth. This thread also runs through his self-analysis shared with his then friend Wilhelm Fliess, which includes several reflections on adolescence more directly. There are numerous links between Freud's adolescence and its aftermath at the end of the 19th century, a time when, according to Anzieu (1959), who mentions self-analysis as the other element at play, Freud was undergoing a midlife crisis (Jacques, 1974) – a crisis that Kleinians see as precisely the end of the adolescent process (Houssier, 2014).

1.5 Between modesty and shame

Freud's relationship to his adolescence and its wounds was probably marked by a certain ambivalence, absent from his memories of childhood, which often include aggressive sexual scenes described without any real censorship. This is not the case with certain dreams, the analysis of which he discreetly interrupts when they pertain to his adolescence. We could speculate that this personal ambivalence, a mixture of modesty and shame, was never overcome and that adolescence remained less elaborated than certain aspects of his childhood, which on the contrary was constantly used as a kind of theoretical compass. As a result, adolescence was generally avoided and appears to have been less of an object of study, with few exceptions – most notably the third essay on sexuality (Freud, 1905a) – which are significant but rarely go beyond mere reminiscences or pedagogical positions, such as concerning the access of young unmarried people to sexuality (Marty and Houssier, 2007). Defending sexual freedom for unmarried youth was part of the context of Freud's theorisation of the anxiety neurosis (Freud, 1895b) and of the theory of sexual frustration as a source of neurotic symptoms. As we shall see, this position in favour of sexuality before marriage also had to do with Freud's own experience of his teenage years, marked by asceticism and sexual repression.

In the perspective of the process of adolescence, one exception was the creation of a psychoanalytical myth of origins, which Freud (1913, 1915, 1925) often related to his early cultural interests, and which I have interpreted as a representation of the confrontation between a father and his adolescent sons (Houssier, 2013a). We should note that the postscript to his *Autobiographical Study* (Freud, 1925) again sees adolescence as one of the sources of his research; having become a psychoanalyst, this return to the cultural problems he had found fascinating as "a youth scarcely old enough for thinking" (Ibid., p. 71) shows us a young man passionate about historical literature and the works of great authors, who used culture as his intermediary, transitional object, like a kind of adolescent version of the idealised stuffed toy.

The fact that Freud maintained his phylogenetic theory until the very end, to give another theoretical example with a cultural significance, also points in this direction: while he did not explicitly theorise the adolescent process, he was sensitive to adolescence in his clinical work, as well as in some of his theory's dark corners.

The question of adolescence therefore has a much more clandestine and discrete presence in Freud's work, which forces us to infer and exhume from the traces left here and there. While writing his work on dream interpretation (Freud, 1900), the alleged founder of neuropaediatrics (Eissler, 2006) explains in a letter to Fliess that he has found the key to adolescent sexual fantasies, and then proceeds to unveil their typical nature in his book: defloration, virginity, seduction fantasies, identification with Christ, a mother who sexually initiates her son to prevent the harmful effects of masturbation and so on. In a letter to Fliess from 30th May 1893, Freud writes about the sexual aetiology of the neuroses:

> I believe I understand the anxiety neuroses of young persons who must be presumed to be virgins and who have not been subjected to abuse. I have analysed two cases of this kind; it was a presentient dread of sexuality, and behind it things they had seen or heard and half-understood – thus, the aetiology is purely emotional but nevertheless of a sexual nature.
>
> (Freud, 1986, p. 49)

This letter was written more than four years before Freud renounced his *Neurotica* in September 1897. The earlier letter seems to prefigure this renouncement and relies on an understanding of certain adolescent cases as a basis for a general aetiology of the neuroses; it describes an imaginary linked to the primitive scene and involving a pubescent curiosity about parental sexuality (noises, struggle, blood, etc.). The internal and phantasmatic dimension of sexual adolescent conflict takes precedence over the theory of sexual abuse, leading to the theorisation of the Oedipus complex, another biographic-theoretical discovery (Freud, 1887–1904, 1900). However, at the time Freud was basically busy with his theory of the neurosis, and his theory of adolescence essentially became reduced to that of hysteria. This absorption and collusion move away from genital sexuality, which was necessary for Freud's argument of the significance of infantile sexuality to the origins of the neurotic symptomatology. Today, these two dimensions can be more easily separated, and we can understand how the clamour of adolescent affectations may have been too often equated with the beginnings of a neurotic illness.

We shall see that Freud's conception of post-pubertal sexuality helped define the "actual neurosis" or that the question of masturbation in adolescence was understood as not only a possible sign of incestuous fixation but also as a continuation of an autoerotic sexuality prone to a detachment from the "real" object of desire. But for the time being, and before getting to the actual material of Freud's biography, let's make a step aside and think about certain elements, significant from the Freudian perspective, of what we now call the process of adolescence.

1.6 Elements of a process

The period of adolescence tends to confront us with the most intense aspects of psychic life, both sexual and destructive. Because infantile conflicts or trauma are revived in adolescence and reinvested by genitality, adolescence is a dynamic psychic transformation. This terminology refers to the title of the third essay on the theory of sexuality, *The Transformations of Puberty* (Freud, 1905a). Adolescent psychoanalysis has always relied on this founding text, together with the Emma case (Freud and Breuer, 1895) and the Dora fragment (Freud, 1905b). The potential psychopathological inflections of adolescence are judged on their transitory or long-lasting nature; this orientation – which way will it tip or, indeed, break out – therefore depends on the adolescent's ability to transform infantile conflicts, against the backdrop of elaborating their partial drives and oedipal attachments. The Oedipus complex, positive or inverted, can only be resolved once it has passed the test of genital maturation, the second stage of a diphasic sexuality.

Until now, the child was protected from fulfilling his incestual and parricidal wishes by his own immaturity; in adolescence, both incest and parricide become possible. For the young person, this is a radically new and complex situation. The process of adolescence is central to the subject's future, not in the same way as the infantile period, but to a comparable degree, given the scale of the subjective construction it mobilises. Among these processes, the paradoxical work of maintaining a link to the parental imagoes clashes with the need to separate oneself from the "real" parents. Two main conflicts have to be worked through, which are indissociable and appear as constitutive in the overcoming of this challenge. The first concerns the post-pubertal specificity of incestual and parricidal wishes and the ability to disengage from them by opening up to the complementarity between the sexes (Birraux and Gutton, 1982); the second has to do with the necessary de-idealisation of the preoedipal same-sex parent, as a condition of a stable identification with which to enter adulthood (Houssier, 2010b).

These psychic aspects go hand in hand with bodily changes. If growing up is inherently an aggressive act (Winnicott, 1971, p. 195), this implies new areas of rivalry previously masked by the child's immaturity. For example, the adolescent becomes able to reproduce and thus gains a new power previously only held by the parents. The parent-child asymmetry is reduced, meaning that the phantasmatic gap between the generations becomes less pronounced. The adolescent acquires certain powers of the same-sex parent and becomes symbolically their potential murderer.

On the sexual level, giving oneself the permission to be sexually active like the parents is a variation on the theme of the novelty of genitality, which requires a new set of identifications. The parental image undergoes a shift, from prohibition to tolerance, which entails a significant modification of the interiorised parent. The adolescent can now picture himself, as well as his parents, as sexually active in reality (Jacobson, 1964), while maintaining the prohibition of incest – two potentially conflicting perspectives.

To unfold the fundamental stakes of this process, we will start from Freud's arguments, both direct and inferred, and open up to current psychoanalytic conceptions.

1.6.1 A Freudian memory: the non-elaboration of adolescent experience in adult treatments

In her discussion of her psychoanalytic work with adolescents, Jeanne Lampl-de Groot (1960) starts with a description of one of Freud's analyses, where he speaks, apropos the importance of reviving adolescence in the treatment, about an adult patient whose analysis progressed without difficulties but also without results. The symptoms only disappeared when the patient, after having discussed her childhood history in great detail, finally uncovered a traumatic experience that occurred in her fifteenth year of life. The elaboration of her trauma involved expressing the related emotions and this authentic working-through was what finally cured her.

This brief clinical example from an informal exchange in the 1930s throws light on both the importance of Freud's work with adolescent patients and the screen-like nature of infantile material, in the sense that, today more than ever, the patient can give the analyst what the latter supposedly wants, that is, stories from the patient's childhood, as a form of defence, in order to silence the lasting pain and intensity of adolescent trauma. Based on her own practice, Lampl-de Groot puts it as follows: adolescence is no longer "only" the screen on which the child's unelaborated infantile sexual and traumatic scenes are replayed, albeit modified by puberty. It becomes a time when certain experiences, combined with the infantile material, can have a comparable and equally determining quality, especially in terms of psychopathology. She also gives us a valuable clue as to the importance, in adult treatments, of the affects involved in elaborating adolescent experience, to some extent contrary to the importance usually given to the function of interpretation. Unsurprisingly, the conclusion she draws from this Vienna memory is that the failure of certain adult treatments has to do with the non-elaboration of adolescent experience (Ibid., p. 103).

Taking a path similar to Winnicott's, she believes that the adolescent's despair is just as devastating as that of the child's and no less profound. The psychological means of grasping these affects are obviously not the same, but the author tilts the balance in an unexpected way. The adult remembers that as an adolescent, he was responsible for his behaviour, he recalls his guilt and shame, his mental conflicts, contradictions and oddities, his unhealed narcissistic wounds. Unlike childhood, adolescence is a period of subjective appropriation, which strengthens the sense of being the only one responsible for one's inner experience. However, the links between adolescence and the infantile take on a particular weight if associated to early relationships.

In fact, there is a certain similarity between adolescents who feel persecuted by precisely what they need, that is, the object or relationship of dependency, and, on the other hand, babies who experience the birth of the object as a necessary yet painful stage, a move from absolute to relative dependency. The object is not given up; we never give up on satisfying our desire for it; instead, we negotiate, as Roussillon writes (Golse and Roussillon, 2010), based on Freud's formula. In other words, we only give up on some of the modalities of satisfying our desire, on certain forms of the object's presence. The negotiation concerns exchanging a prior mode of satisfaction, which is impossible or prohibited, for one that is compatible with the present situation. Adolescence comes as a marker of the infantile which is revived and transformed, and then again repressed; as adults, we no longer remember our adolescence. This double caesura of repression, coming after infantile amnesia, shows us the importance of treating adolescents in order to best prepare the potential adult neurosis.

1.6.2 Significant occurrences in Freudian theory

In adolescence, the source of powerful fantasies is primarily the genitalisation of the body. The sense of familiarity with oneself and one's body is undermined; the young person suddenly becomes a stranger to himself and those around him. The collapse of the boundary between the actual and the repressed blurs the lines between the imaginary and reality and confronts the adolescent with an enigma.

The influx of the drives at puberty and their potentially disorganising effects share certain similarities with the feeling of the uncanny. In his definition, Freud (1919) reminds us of the meaning of the German word *Unheimlich*: something hidden, secret, which should remain in the shadows but instead comes to light – in the adolescent case, the possible fulfilment of murderous and incestuous desires. Freud understands the uncanny via primary narcissism, describing a time when "the ego had not yet marked itself off sharply from the external world and from other people" (Freud, 1919, p. 236). The train of new sensations experienced in the adolescent body revives much earlier experience, not only pregenital but also primitive, as shown by current research on the links between the experience of babies and adolescents (Golse and Roussillon, 2010). Schur (1972) highlights that Freud, while living as a young man alone in a foreign city, would often hear his name suddenly called by a familiar and beloved voice. He would note down the exact moment of this hallucination, in order to ask his family if something had happened at that precise time. "The attitude of Freud's was understandable: he himself had discovered things which had been scorned as wild fantasies by the academic world", Schur argues (Ibid., p. 252).

The loss of familiarity is characteristic of this now foreign body, which has become unknown before it can be reintegrated. Not feeling "at home" can also be linked to the adolescent's sense of being drawn towards non-incestual figures outside the family. While taking into account its infantile roots, "genuine" mental anorexia can be considered as the negative of the adolescent process (Houssier, 2011a). In terms of psychopathology, while depersonalisation concerns adolescents who are struggling but able to regress, im-personalisation is a sign of abandoning the other in oneself, the stranger within. Mental anorexia provides a paradigmatic illustration of a body that has become an intimate enemy. It shows us the subjective impasses of the process, manifested in a mental action upon the body, where puberty and its effects have revealed that a certain psychic threshold could not be elaborated. The nullification of the body is accompanied by a withdrawal because any object-relation triggers anxiety. The im-personalisation of relationships in anorexia is connected to a de-corporation, on the level of fantasy, which puts pressure on the connections between the body and the ego. When the ego feels its unity threatened, the subject tries to maintain a sense of inner cohesion via primary psychic mechanisms. In terms of psychopathology, the fantasies of a joint body, of close physical contact or adhesive identification illustrate the depths of the identity reconstruction in adolescence. The unconscious fantasies of undifferentiation are indicative of both the challenges of this process and the impasse in appropriating the unity of psyche and soma.

But let us return to Freud: the *heim* in *Unheimlich* means "what is part of the home and the family". One possible translation is therefore "unhomely". Laplanche (1989) argues that at the onset of puberty, infantile sexuality is already in place. The specificity of adolescence is therefore being confronted with the new genital paradigm while infantile sexuality is "already there". This explains why adolescents experience their bodies as uncanny, as someone they are not, or at least not yet. Genital sexuality is a stranger intruding in the young person's body and psyche; this intrusion is compounded by the growing intensity of the drive post puberty, which in some circumstances may overwhelm the psyche's capacities of containment. This unstoppable quota of excitation creates a potential for internal trauma throughout adolescence.

1.6.3 Escaping parental authority, between idealisation and murder

Based on the idea of the uncanny as an experience of the adolescent body, we could offer the following definition of adolescence: a work of subjectivation, of somatic and psychic appropriation, which consists in making familiar what has become strange and unknown. This process of re-familiarisation involves an elaboration, through familiarisation, of incestual and parricidal wishes. Overall, the process promotes the possibility of psychic life with a tolerable level of conflict. The opposition or polarity between the strange and the familiar that underpins the adolescent experience resonates with Winnicott's idea of the sense of being real; it affects the most intimate sphere of existence and touches on the issues of identity characteristic of the adolescent journey, against the backdrop of fears of invasion by de-structuring fantasies. The latter are relegated to the ego's fringes, often using archaic defence mechanisms and showing that the enemy in adolescence is the body and its new capacities for orgiastic enjoyment (Birraux, 1980). This capacity gives rise to anxiety-producing fantasies such as the fear of castration, of bodily damage or the fear of an enjoyment that is both uncontrolled and uncontrollable. Fantasies experienced as terrifying are combined with a deeper and unspeakable anxiety: the ego's fear of disintegration, the anguish of primitive helplessness and of collapse when faced with the demands of the external world.

Freud (1905a) speaks about the challenges specific to these changes: "One of the most significant, but also one of the most painful, psychical achievements of the pubertal period" consists in a "detachment from parental authority" (Ibid., p. 226). This task implies a gradual de-sensualisation of the attachments to parental and fraternal figures.

Contrary to incestuous desires, the death wishes directed at the same-sex parent remain in the sphere of fantasy and are not meant to be realised (Houssier, 2010a). Pubertal sexual life must therefore initially be limited to "indulging in phantasies", "in ideas that are not destined to be carried into effect" (p. 225). This phantasmatic activity centred on object-choice can become a fixation. The infantile dimension of the chosen fantasy scenario fuels this fixation via fantasy activity, highlighting one of the key challenges of adolescence – moving from a wish enacted in fantasy to its fulfilment with an external object.

When at last he stood at the Acropolis, which his father had never visited, Freud (1936) spoke about the fulfilment of an adolescent dream. He analysed his strange feelings as a return of an internal refusal, of having gone further than his father. This symbolic murder indicates that in order to be accepted without castration returning in the uncanny, one must be able to criticise one's father, to reduce his power while one's own strength increases, and free oneself of this guilt in order to enjoy the good things in life – a murderous-critical thought process, which the persisting idealisation of paternal imagoes tends to inhibit (Houssier, 2012).

Adolescence is again mentioned when Freud (1921) talks about the overvaluing of the sexual object. The introduction of the concept of narcissism helps him develop the link between tenderness and sensuality; the adolescent who overvalues the love-object invests a part of his own narcissism in it; this idealisation leads the ego to abandon itself in and be absorbed by the object. This murder of the ego's critical abilities leads to an idea of the object replacing the ego ideal, reminding us of the idolatrous idealisations of adolescence as a prefiguration of the adolescent neurosis, or of the more regressive aspects of adolescence where the ego becomes conflated with the primary object. The libidinal changes that strive to reorganise the relationship with parents include a period of transitory disinvestment of the values and prohibitions connected to parental figures. This in turn brings in the idea of a transgressive potential, universal to adolescence and inherent to the dynamic of regression mobilised by the adolescent process. The disinvestment or counter-investment of the parental values and prohibitions are part of the fantasy attacks on the parental imagoes, a critical attitude required to elaborate the feelings of hatred and destructiveness towards the object.

In adolescence, the powerful sensual current no longer ignores the sexual genital aim, which combines with tender fixations, the aim-inhibited drives that mark a halt to the dynamic of direct sexual satisfaction. We see the specific temporality of the adolescent process: the delay between psychic and physical sexual maturity leaves a gap in object-relations. This manifests, for example, in the role that affection plays in teenage friendships, something that Freud experienced himself with Eduard Silberstein (Houssier, 2013b). Having set the context and established the link between life and work, let us now take a closer look at the realities of this troubled youth.

Bibliography

Anzieu D. (1959), *L'auto-analyse de Freud*, Paris, PUF.

Birraux A. (1980), *L'adolescent face à son corps*, Paris, Editions universitaires.

Birraux A., Gutton P. (1982), Ils virent qu'ils étaient nus. Différence et complémentarité des sexes à l'adolescence, *Psychanalyse à l'université*, 7, p. 671–679.

De Mijolla A. (1996), Un adolescent bien tranquille: S. Freud, *Les Cahiers du Collège International de l'Adolescence*, 1, p. 231–267.

De Mijolla A. (2003), *Freud. Fragments d'une histoire*, Paris, PUF.

Eissler K. R. (1978), Creativity and adolescence: the effect of trauma in Freud's adolescence, *The Psychoanalytic Study of the Child*, 33, p. 461–518.

Eissler K. R. (2006), Esquisse biographique, in Eissler K., Freud E., Freud L., Grubitch Simitis I., Fleckhaus W. (dir.), *Sigmund Freud. Lieux, visages, objets*, Paris, Gallimard, p. 10–38.

Freud A. (1958), Adolescence, *Psychoanalytic Study of the Child*, 13, p. 255–278.

Freud S. (1877, 1994), Observation de la conformation de l'organe lobé de l'anguille décrit comme glande germinale mâle, in Fédida P., Widlöcher D. (dir.), *Les évolutions phylogénétiques de l'individuation*, Paris, PUF, p. 9–20.

Freud S. (1895a, 1956), *La naissance de la psychanalyse*, Paris, PUF.

Freud S. (1895b, 1894), The justification for detaching from neurasthenia a particular syndrome: The anxiety-neurosis. *Collected Papers*. Vol. I. New York, Basic Books, p. 76–106.

Freud S. (ed.). (1900), *The Interpretation of Dreams*. SE 4, London, Hogarth Press, p. ix–627.

Freud S. (1904a, 2006), En mémoire du Professeur S. Hammerschlag, in *Oeuvre complètes*, VI, Paris, PUF, p. 41.

Freud S. (1904b), *Obituary of Professor S. Hammerschlag from Contributions to the Neue Freie Presse*. SE 9, London, Hogarth Press, p. 255–256.

Freud S. (1905a), *Three Essays on the Theory of Sexuality*. SE 7, London, Hogarth Press, p. 123–246.

Freud S. (1905b), *Fragment of an Analysis of a Case of Hysteria (1905 [1901])*. SE 7, London, Hogarth Press, p. 1–122.

Freud S. (1913), *Totem and Taboo: Some Points of Agreement between the Mental Lives of Savages and Neurotics (1913 [1912–13])*. SE 13, London, Hogarth Press, p. vii–162.

Freud S. (1915, 1986), *Vues d'ensemble sur les névroses de transfert*, Paris, Gallimard.

Freud S. (1919), *The 'Uncanny'*. SE 17, London, Hogarth Press, p. 217–256.

Freud S. (1921), *Group Psychology and the Analysis of the Ego*. SE 18, London, Hogarth Press, p. 65–144.

Freud S. (1925), *An Autobiographical Study*. SE 20, London, Hogarth Press, p. 1–70.

Freud S. (1936), *A Disturbance of Memory on the Acropolis*. SE 22, London, Hogarth Press, p. 237–248.

Freud S. (1986), *The Complete Letters to Wilhelm Fliess (1887–1904)*, Cambridge, MA, Harvard University Press.

Freud S. (1990), *Lettres de jeunesse (1871–1881)*, Paris, Gallimard.

Freud S., Breuer J. (1895), *Studies on Hysteria*. SE 2, London, Hogarth Press, p. ix–310.

Gedo J., Wolf E. (1970), Die Ichthyosaurusbriefe, *Psyche*, 24, p. 785–797.

Golse B., Roussillon R. (2010), *La naissance de l'objet*, Paris, PUF.

Gutton P. (2004), Une création à l'Université: l'Unité de Recherches Adolescence, *Recherches en psychanalyse*, 1, p. 21–26.

Houssier F. (2010a), *Anna Freud et son école. Créativité et controverses*, Paris, Campagne-Première.

Houssier F. (2010b), Peter Blos, une oeuvre consacrée au processus d'adolescence, in Givre P., Tassel A. (sous la direction de), *Le tourment adolescent*. Tome 2, Paris, PUF, p. 51–83.

Houssier F. (2011a), Positions psychotiques dans la cure d'une adolescente anorexique, in F. Marty (sous la dir. de), *Psychopathologie de l'adolescent: 10 cas cliniques*, Paris, In Press, p. 213–233.

Houssier F. (2011b), S. Freud et son Antigone: adolescence et liens de mutualité théoriques, *Topique*, 115, p. 17–32.

Houssier F. (2012), Vœux parricides et fantasmes de dévoration. De la désidéalisation du père à l'adolescence, *Psychiatrie de l'enfant*, LV, 2, p. 563–579.

Houssier F. (2013a), *Meurtres dans la famille*, Paris, Dunod.

Houssier F. (2013b), Sigmund Freud/Eduard Silberstein: une amitié passionnelle et consanguine, *Adolescence*, 83, 31(1), p. 219–226.

Houssier F. (2014), Sauvagerie et confusion: l'adolescence dans le courant post-kleinien, *Topique*, 217, p. 79–93.

Houssier F. (2016), Entre S. Freud et S. Ferenczi, un Œdipe pubertaire?, *Les lettres de la SPF*, 35, p. 157–173.

Houssier F. (2019), *Freud étudiant*, Paris, Campagne-Première.

Houssier F., Christaki A. (2016), Folie pubertaire et sexualité diabolique dans les débuts de la psychanalyse, *Topique*, 134, p. 157–170.

Houssier F., Vlachopoulou X. (2015), Winnicott entre dedans et dehors. Extraits de correspondance, *Adolescence*, 33(4), p. 911–923.

Huber G. (2009), *Si c'était Freud*, Lormond, Le bord de l'eau.

Jacobson E. (1964, 1975), *Le Soi et le monde objectal*, Paris, PUF.

Jacques E. (1974), Mort et vie dans la crise du milieu de vie, in Anzieu D. (dir.), *Psychanalyse du génie créateur*, Paris, Dunod, p. 238–260.

Jones E. (1958, 2006), *La vie et l'œuvre de S. Freud, T. 1: La jeunesse de Freud (1856–1900)*, Paris, PUF.

Klumpner G. H. (1978), A hypothesis regarding the origins of Freud's concepts of the psychology of adolescence, *Annual of Psychoanalysis*, 6, p. 3–22.

Lampl-de Groot J. (1960, 1997), De l'adolescence, in Perret-Catipovic M., Ladame F. (dir.), *Adolescence et psychanalyse: une histoire*, Lausanne, Delachaux et Niestlé, p. 101–112.

Laplanche J. (1989), *New Foundations for Psychoanalysis*, Hoboken, NJ, Wiley & Sons.

Marty F. (dir.). (2002), *Le jeune délinquant*, Paris, Payot.

Marty F., Houssier F. (dir.). (2007), Eduquer l'adolescent? in *Pour une pédagogie psychanalytique*, Nîmes, Editions Champ Social.

Pontalis J.-B. (1976), Introduction, in *Les premiers psychanalystes. Minutes de la société psychanalytique de Vienne*, Paris, Gallimard, p. 4–5.

Rodrigué E. (2000), Freud. *Le siècle de la psychanalyse*, T. 1, Paris, Payot.

Schur M. (1972), *Freud: Living and Dying*, Cambridge, International University Press.

Winnicott D. W. (1971, 2005), *Playing and Reality*, London, Taylor & Francis.

Chapter 2

Infantile traces and first connections

Freud's biography cannot be separated from the milieu in which he was raised. In this sense, the mid-19th-century rise of the natural sciences and positivism, as well as the Jewish emancipation movement spurring an unprecedented access to culture and academia, constituted the indispensable external conditions that allowed Freud to conceive of and create psychoanalysis. For example, the political emancipation of Austrian Jews which came into effect after 1866 in part fuelled the fulfilment of his dreams of greatness.

Freud grew up in a period of liberalism when Vienna was the centre of scientific and intellectual influence. Its liberal political leaders opposed the power of the Catholic Church and anti-Semitism but supported the Austrian monarchy. The education reform had an impact on secondary-school teaching, promoting respect for the dignity and uniqueness of man. Freud benefited from these humanistic tendencies, which permeated both the theory and practice of psychoanalysis (Ticho and Ticho, 1972).

Freud's environment was also marked by the spread of diseases such as tuberculosis, by the struggle for nourishment linked to poverty or by promiscuity. Things that appear more dispersed, such as the influence of his Jewishness, will only be part of our reflection, though often they would deserve a more detailed discussion. At the same time, we will focus on Freud's early environment, his family and the specificities of his first object-relations, which again returned to the fore in adolescence.

2.1 Return to origins

Freud was born into a unique family context: he was his father's youngest child, then became the oldest of his siblings. He was preceded by two older half-brothers from his father's first marriage. His nephew John and niece Pauline were therefore practically his peers. His young mother was of the same generation as his half-brothers, while his father Jacob could have been his grandfather. Jacob was also the grandfather of Freud's nephew John (Bernfeld, 1944).

Freud's father Jacob moved to Freiberg at the age of twenty-five. Sigismund was a lively child, growing up harmoniously. In the workshop of the locksmith

DOI: 10.4324/9781003340898-2

Zajic, with whom the Freuds shared the first floor of a local house, his joie de vivre and creativity manifested in making toys out of scrap metal (Eissler, 2006). Jacob had previously married at sixteen and had had two children, Emanuel and Philipp; after the death of his first wife he remarried, but his new wife died soon after their wedding. He entered into his third marriage, to Amalia, in 1855; she was twenty, while Jacob was forty. Jacob's father died two months before Sigismund's birth and in addition to his German first name, the child was also given the Jewish first name of his grandfather, Salomon, meaning "the wise".

Hence, in addition to the deaths of Jacob's first two wives, his grandfather Schlomo also passed away before Sigismund's arrival; Amalia then lost another baby, Julius, when Sigismund was eleven months old. Breger (2000) highlights this series of deaths to emphasise the mournful atmosphere of Sigismund's earliest years, leaving him vulnerable and terrified, at a time when he could not make sense of this deadly climate. The author speaks about a fear of death while his mother was preoccupied by new babies, which was true throughout his childhood, given that he was the eldest of six children born roughly every other year. Moreover, he may have associated his mother's absences with tuberculosis; the fear of losing those he relied on most was linked to the primary fear of losing his mother, through her absence or death. At the age of eight or nine (Freud, 1900), he had a dream while his mother was away from home. In the dream, she appeared to him looking peculiarly peaceful, her face softened by sleep. She was carried into the room by people with bird's beaks and laid on the bed. He woke up from this nightmare screaming and crying; in his book on dreams, he connects these ideas with a funeral. These elements are combined with the death of his grandfather, whose face bore the same expression as his mother's face in the dream; Freud could see it as his grandfather lay snoring in a coma shortly before his death. This mixing of generations in the family relationships condensates and combines together a woman and a man, which will later return in the bi-sexed representations of women, especially his fiancée Martha. The grandfather's image linked to that of his mother is not without importance; it belongs to a series of elements that suggest that Freud's attacks on the figure of the father and especially his substitutes partially concealed his hostile feelings against his mother (Abraham, 1982), the way a father takes on the hatred of the earliest childhood previously centred on the baby's mother.

This mother, constantly occupied by other young children, is seen as a source of anxiety and resentment for Freud. While his relationship with his mother probably received less attention than his relationship to his father, he was able to reconstruct his feelings of guilt towards his brother Julius; just like any other child, he felt a rivalry with the new-born and a wish to get rid of him. In his self-analysis, Freud (1887–1904) wrote to Fliess that Julius' death left behind a grain of self-reproach, while at the same time subtracting the feelings of betrayal due to Amalia's repeated pregnancies and his ardent desire to be loved by his mother.

The period before leaving for Vienna includes another important character of Freud's early history. During his dream analysis (Freud, 1900), he remembered the nanny who took care of him until he was two and a half years old. While he only had vague memories of this person, his self-analysis led him to find out more from his mother, who described the nursemaid as old and ugly, but also intelligent and efficient. He writes: "Her treatment of me was not always excessive in its amiability and her words could be harsh if I failed to reach the required standard of cleanliness" (Freud, 1900, p. 247). Nevertheless, Freud concludes that he must have loved this prehistoric old nurse, his first "educator", whose image blends with that of his mother.

Freud's analysis of his screen memories corroborates the idea of a loss of his mother following her new pregnancy; his early experiences with his mother and nanny appear both complementary and interchangeable. He tells Fliess the following story: as a child, one day he couldn't find his mother and was screaming desperately. His half-brother Philipp opened an empty "box" (cupboard); his mother then appeared at the door, looking "slim and beautiful" (Freud, 1887–1904, p. 263). In Freud's memories the mother's idealised image remains, while at the same time he fears the disappearance of his nanny. Faced with the challenge of loss, his mother appears in all her ideal splendour: beautiful, not pregnant, in a scene where the nanny is simultaneously linked to culpability and theft. Having taken several precious objects from the Freuds, including some of Sigismund's toys, the nursemaid was reported to the police by his half-brother Emmanuel and arrested, "boxed up", for theft (p. 264). His "Nannie", he writes to Fliess in 1897, his teacher in sexual matters, also washed him in reddish water in which she had herself previously bathed and was reprimanded for this, her fault bringing together sexuality and punishment in young Freud's imagination.

But that is not all. Just like in his letter to Rolland (Freud, 1936), the writing of these lines to Fliess at the age of forty-one brings up another puzzling memory, one that has been tormenting him for twenty-five years. The dream about his nursemaid, which led him to question his mother, reminded him that his Nannie suddenly disappeared from his life, but also that he should remember her, based on a scene that was remembered when he was sixteen. At the beginning of psychoanalysis, Freud's idea was that the memories that re-emerge in adolescence allow us to find traces of infantile memories or impressions. Adolescence carried the memory of the infantile; it created mnesic shortcuts to the past, turning the young person into a historian of oneself and one's family (Houssier, 2013b). The age of sixteen is also when the wave of repression linked to the decline of the Oedipus complex and the onset of the latency stage tends to ebb back, "leaking" certain memories. This porosity of repression is indirectly illustrated by Freud when he speaks, in a clinical vignette of a young female patient, about "an unconscious phantasy dating from puberty" (1900, p. 569): a wish to be continuously pregnant and have a great many children is later combined with a desire to have these children with as many lovers as possible.

However, another more nuanced idea emerges, of a loss shared by mother and son and introducing an emotional distance between them. Disagreeably and disappointingly, the distant mother replaces the sexualised figures of the mother and the nursemaid. In the story of the "box", the mother appears slim and beautiful, as if revived; her radiating presence brings together the sexualised mother and the idealised one, leading towards an oedipal position (Hardin, 1987). His mother is associated with grief, death and disease, while his nanny is linked to crime and guilt. Freud's son Martin (1958) describes his grandmother Amalia as an untameable, aggressive and affected woman, who was rather insensitive to the feelings of others and determined to make her own way in life. Her vitality and impatience combined with the fact Freud's sister Adolfina (Dolfi) became her mother's life companion and caretaker.

Martin Freud also describes his grandmother as a tornado, a charming domestic tyrant. Freud's biographers have mainly seen his memories of his mother as a screen against the early loss of his nanny. One element nonetheless suggests the formula might be reversed. In a letter to Martha Bernays from 1883, Freud writes about a painting in a Dresden museum (Freud, 1873–1939, p. 81): "Raphael's Madonna [. . .] is a girl, say sixteen years old; she gazes out on the world with such a fresh and innocent expression." He adds that the idea that came to his mind was that this young girl was a "charming, sympathetic nursemaid, not from the celestial world but from ours". In the story, his friends reject the idea, instead finding the image of the virgin to be a true Madonna. To the idea of a young virgin, Freud associates the image of an idealised and then de-idealised nursemaid, with a more direct erotic potential. The mother and the nursemaid are thus much less clearly differentiated and in fact interchangeable, so that the final representation combines different elements, bringing together sexuality, loss and abandonment. The image of the mother-nursemaid double becomes thus a combined representation of the mother of the earliest years in Freiberg. Like all subjects that matter in Freud's thought, adolescence too passes through a metaphor. Freud associates a girl in her teens with the figure of the Madonna; there is a fantasy of parthenogenesis, in the idea of a virgin bearing a child. She also represents a young girl's proclivity for sexual guilt.

> A first suspicion of this connection came to me while I was working as a physician at the Psychiatric Clinic of the University. I there came across a case of confusional insanity with hallucinations, in which the attack [. . .] turned out to be a reaction to a reproach made against the patient by her fiancé.
>
> (1905, p. 103, n2)

But let's return to Freud's own childhood. At the age of three, his experience of leaving Freiberg for Vienna by train, a difficult moment marked by a loss, left him with a phobia of train travel. Freud later wrote about the terrifying lights that made him think of souls burning in hell, linking religious imagery with the loss of his nanny, who had lectured him on the Almighty's power and hell. His infantile phobia revolved specifically around the idea of the train departing without him, of being abandoned, losing his mother and father after he had already lost his nanny, his hometown and the familiarity of his earliest environment.

The oedipal component is brought up more clearly when he writes: "If a man has been his mother's undisputed darling he retains throughout life the triumphant feeling, the confidence in success, which not seldom brings actual success along with it" (1917, p. 155). This fragment of self-analysis is not only defensive vis-à-vis preoedipal challenges. It reveals an important element of Freud's psychic life, which, after having re-emerged and intensified in adolescence, became the fundamental driver of his ambitions. Since his birth, he had been Amalia's pride, her "golden Sigi" – a nickname highlighting his mother's favouritism and her conviction of his glorious future. Amalia's belief was reinforced by an encounter at a bakery, where an old woman announced to her that her son was a genius (Roudinesco, 2014). Freud himself would dismiss these as the prophecies of old women, who look into the future to compensate for the loss of their status in the present (Freud, 1900).

Nevertheless, Amelia shared her passion with Jacob, who also began to admire his son and believe he might surpass him one day (Bernfeld, 1944). And that is not all – Freud (1900) remembers another scene, wondering: "Could this have been the source of my thirst for grandeur?" (p. 191).

> But that reminded me of another experience, dating from my later childhood, which provided a still better explanation. My parents had been in the habit, when I was a boy of eleven or twelve, of taking me with them to the Prater. One evening, while we were sitting in a restaurant there, our attention had been attracted by a man who was moving from one table to another and, for a small consideration, improvising a verse upon any topic presented to him. I was despatched to bring the poet to our table and he showed his gratitude to the messenger. Before enquiring what the chosen topic was to be, he had dedicated a few lines to myself; and he had been inspired to declare that I should probably grow up to be a Cabinet Minister.
>
> (p. 191–192)

This prophecy was associated with the era of the *Bürger* ministry. Freud's father brought home the portraits of different politicians – Herbst, Giskra, Unger, Berger – including several Jews. Freud remembers that every industrious Jewish schoolboy carried such a portfolio in his school bag.

> The events of that period no doubt had some bearing on the fact that up to a time shortly before I entered the University it had been my intention to study Law; it was only at the last moment that I changed my mind. A ministerial career is definitely barred to a medical man
>
> (Ibid.)

he concludes in the same spirit.

2.2 Checkmate

Freud's father Jacob had been a practicing Jew, but over time he became a free thinker. He was unable to keep his father's wool business going; after this professional failure, moving to Vienna was the only option, a search for a fresh start. However, there too Jacob never quite succeeded and had to repeatedly seek help from his family and friends. As we shall see, this Achilles' heel became an important element of Freud's ambivalence towards his father, which seeped into his inner life and dreams. Father's inability to provide for his family's present and future was part of the story of paternal weakness (Roudinesco, 2014), which we can understand as a highly ambivalent attitude in the sense of a symbolic murder of the paternal figure, inherent to the boy's process of adolescence.

Still, what little he had in Freiberg Jacob lost to the financial crisis of 1873, both financially and professionally. While he hoped for his eldest son to go into business, he did not stand in the way of Sigmund's professional ambitions. Apropos Freiberg, Freud described one of his dreams, the dream of the "one-eyed doctor", in which he started developing what later became the concept of displacement:

> At this point I may mention a dream of my own, in which what had to be traced was not an impression but a connection. I had a dream of someone who I knew in my dream was the doctor in my native town. His face was indistinct, but was confused with a picture of one of the masters at my secondary school, whom I still meet occasionally. When I woke up I could not discover what connection there was between these two men. I made some enquiries from my mother, however, about this doctor who dated back to the earliest years of my childhood, and learnt that he had only one eye. The schoolmaster whose figure had covered that of the doctor in the dream, was also one-eyed. It was thirty-eight years since I had seen the doctor, and so far as I know I had never thought of him in my waking life.
>
> (Freud, 1900, p. 16)

A new meaning emerges when we learn that the doctor, Josef Pur, later became the mayor of Freiberg. This political undertone was not without interest for Freud, who in his teenage years briefly considered a ministerial career.

In his letter to the mayor in 1931, Freud said that he had left his hometown at the age of three and only came back once, at the age of sixteen, to spend his school holidays in the family of Ignaz Fluss. He never again returned. Speaking about this period of his youth and his encounter with Gisela Fluss (Freud, 1899), he would add a year to his age, while in fact he had been fifteen.

The Freuds met the Fluss family, who were also Jewish, probably through Ignaz Fluss, who was also in the textile business. Jacob Freud's professional failure could be blamed on anti-Semitism and the financial crisis of the 1850s, but these reasons did not quite hold in the local and more favourable context. During the same period, Ignaz Fluss did very well in Freiberg, despite the fact that his situation was not dissimilar to Jacob's, thus challenging the idea that Freud's father was "crushed by an unavoidable economic process" (Eissler, 1978, p. 463).

Freud's main teenage love interest, Gisela Fluss, did not remain his only love-object. The portrait he painted in his letters to Eduard Silberstein shows that in the family romance imagined by him, Gisela's mother and father were also highly idealised as the intelligent and successful substitute parents (Houssier, 2015). While Freud mostly emphasised his oedipal love for Gisela's mother, he could not possibly have been indifferent to the image of a father who had succeeded where his own had failed.

Jacob Freud appears to have been a warm and pleasant man, covering over the idea of a father unable to protect his young son from poverty and life's tribulations. The memory of rivalrous games with his nephew John tends to dilute Sigmund's rivalry with his father, which nonetheless appears in dream analysis or in the guilt felt towards his brother Julius, who passed away before his birth. In a context triangulated by the presence of his niece Pauline, Freud returns to the memory of this direct rivalry with John as a model for his ambivalence in his friendships. In this relational dynamic, any friend simultaneously becomes an enemy. Bernfeld (1944) also believes that this figure of the "frenemy" enshrines Freud's early friendships with John and Pauline and remains one of the leitmotifs of his life, from childhood to adulthood. At the same time, his feelings towards his mother were never elaborated to the same degree.

The departure of Freud's half-brothers for England took away his memories of the games played with John and Pauline, to which he then returned in his paper on screen-memories, one of his most autobiographical texts, largely coloured by the reminiscences of his youth (Freud, 1899). Freud's admiration for England was also linked to the stability and success of Jacob's brothers, Emanuel and Philipp, who could send money to his father and the family. In a letter to his fiancée Martha Bernays, he writes:

> Yesterday I met Father in the street, still full of projects, still hoping. I took it upon myself to write to Emanuel and Philipp urging them to help Father out of his present predicament. He doesn't want to do it himself since he considers himself badly treated. So I sat down last night and wrote Emanuel a very sharp letter.

> (1873–1939, p. 86)

Another link with his adolescence has to do with Freud's friendship with Eduard Silberstein. The central theme of his quasi-tyrannical fits of anger directed at Eduard was Freud's worry about the reciprocity of their friendship; he deeply resented his friend's absences and passionately reproached him for his irregular letters (Houssier, 2013c). The source of their relationship was a mixture of two central – and deeply ambivalent – figures of Freud's childhood, namely his father and his nephew John.

2.3 The first link between childhood and adolescence: the "frenemy"

Freud returned to this ambivalence in the dream of "non vixit". The dream associations sparked several memories, which he organises in a regressive order.
The most recent one concerns a reproach for being late coming from Professor
Brücke, an eminent neurophysiologist and an important paternal figure, in whose
laboratory Freud worked as an assistant (Freud, 1900, p. 234). The character
named Josef – probably Josef Paneth, one of his teenage friends – who anni-
hilates him in the dream, represents a link between the figures of Brücke and
Freud's father. Here Freud describes his relationship with his nephew John, who
was a year older than him: "Until the end of my third year we had been inseparable. We had loved each other and fought with each other; and this childhood
relationship [. . .] had a determining influence on all my subsequent relations with
contemporaries" (Ibid., p. 423).

This foray into childhood draws a line of continuity between his friendships
and the relationship with his father. As he suggests, the picture is also imbued
with a sense of loss: "All my friends have in a certain sense been re-incarnations
of this first figure who ['. . . long since appeared before my troubled gaze']: they
have been revenants." To complete the tableau of his childhood, he adds a link
with his teenage years:

> My nephew himself re-appeared in my boyhood, and at that time we acted
> the parts of Caesar and Brutus together. My emotional life has always insisted
> that I should have an intimate friend and a hated enemy. I have always been
> able to provide myself afresh with both, and it has not infrequently happened
> that the ideal situation of childhood has been so completely reproduced that
> friend and enemy have come together in a single individual.
>
> (Freud, 1900, p. 482)

– a fact that his life journey confirmed again and again.

In his analysis, Freud does not decide whether the memory is real or a fantasy;
both are closely tied together. He reconstructs the entire scene of rivalry with John
as follows: two children are arguing over an object, each of them claiming to have
been the first to arrive and thus having a legitimate right to possess it.

> However, this time I was the stronger and remained in possession of the
> field. The vanquished party hurried to his grandfather – my father – and com-
> plained about me, and I defended myself in the words which I know from my
> father's account: "I hit him 'cos he hit me.'"
>
> (p. 482–483)

Later, Freud highlights the dream's latent thoughts: "'It serves you right if you
had to make way for me. Why did you try to push me out of the way? I don't
need you, I can easily find someone else to play with,' and so on" (Ibid.). The

substitutability of friends as parental substitutes articulates the displacement in dreams as well as the sliding of masculine libidinal investments. At the same time, this apparent elasticity cannot hide the passionate nature of the attachment, as the relationship with Silverstein showed in all its harshness.

This first outline sets out a panorama of all object-relations: on the female side, a more fixed cathexis connects his mother and his nanny with Martha, a line briefly crossed, in adolescence, by his fleeting passion for Gisela Fluss and her mother; on the male side, a line of continuity starting from his father and John, where the relationship with the latter is especially strongly present in Freud's friendship with Eduard and later extends to Fliess and Ferenczi (Houssier, 2016), among others.

2.4 Vienna, *terra ambivalente*

Jacob's fiasco in Freiburg and the move to Vienna have been described as the original catastrophe disrupting Freud's life. The world of his three earliest years had two defining characteristics: first, his extended family, which became a recurrent model of the familial space for both Freud and his daughter Anna (Houssier, 2010); second, the shattering of this unified world, which resulted in a series of losses, of his relationships with John and Pauline, as well as his half-brothers Emanuel and Philipp.

The birth of Freud's sister Anna provoked a more conscious feeling of hostility, contrary to his younger sisters, to whom he felt emotionally closer. He was constantly confronted with new births, until the arrival of his youngest brother Alexander when Freud was ten, which Breger (2000) interprets as a non-integration of early traumatic experience. When Freud would return to his memories of this time, he would speak about it lightly: in his recollections, Freiberg is idealised like the mother of the earliest days, magnified before she inhabits a more ambivalent context. This tendency is patent in certain theoretical texts, for example the essays on the psychology of love or on femininity (Freud, 1910–1918, 1931b), which highlight the original attachment to the mother alongside hostile and at times genuinely hateful feelings.

Vienna was therefore an object of displacement, of love and hate, while Freiberg remained idealised, and the emotions attached to the two cities were freely expressed in his letters to Silberstein (Freud, 1871–1881). Amalia and later Jacob gave him lessons and taught him how to read and write. Freud loved his father telling him stories from the Bible, like a genealogical family romance. Later, these stories nurtured his admiration for ancient Egypt, especially the figures of Moses, Samson, Saul, David and Jacob, in whom he found some of the traits of his own family, with multiple marriages leading to a large progeny. By imagining his half-brother Philipp, in Freiberg, as his mother's husband and his father as his grandfather, Freud found himself attached to a seductive and exclusive mother. The construction of this family romance drew on these ancient images, as evidenced by the nightmare in which he saw his mother sleeping and carried onto her bed by bird-beaked figures, direct references to the Egyptian divinities depicted in the family Bible.

At the age of nine, after perhaps having attended a private elementary school, the name of which remains unknown to us, Freud successfully passed the entrance exam for the Leopoldstadt Gymnasium. The much-commented on dream of the "Three Fates" gives us a few more details:

> When I was six years old and was given my first lessons by my mother, I was expected to believe that we were all made of earth and must therefore return to earth. This did not suit me and I expressed doubts of the doctrine. My mother thereupon rubbed the palms of her hands together – just as she did in making dumplings, except that there was no dough between them – and showed me the blackish scales of epidermis produced by the friction as a proof that we were made of earth. My astonishment at this ocular demonstration knew no bounds and I acquiesced in the belief which I was later to hear expressed in the words: *"Du bist der Natur einen Tod sckuldig."* ["Thou owest Nature a death."] So they really were Fates that I found in the kitchen when I went into it – as I had so often done in my childhood when I was hungry, while my mother, standing by the fire, had admonished me that I must wait till dinner was ready.
>
> (Freud, 1900, p. 204)

2.5 Humiliation, between father and son

In the book on dreams, Freud identifies two other memories that left a mark on him (1900, p. 254). In the dream of "Count Thun", he recalls an indirect memory. He would often ask his mother for information, although he does not say so this time:

> It appears that when I was two years old I still occasionally wetted the bed, and when I was reproached for this I consoled my father by promising to buy him a nice new red bed in N., the nearest town of any size.

Freud attributes the promise made to his father to infantile megalomania, adding that in adult neurosis, enuresis and ambition appear closely linked.

This first memory brings back another, more familiar to the historians of psychoanalysis:

> When I was seven or eight years old there was another domestic scene, which I can remember very clearly. One evening before going to sleep I disregarded the rules which modesty lays down and obeyed the calls of nature in my parents' bedroom while they were present. In the course of his reprimand, my father let fall the words: "The boy will come to nothing." This must have been a frightful blow to my ambition, for references to this scene are still constantly recurring in my dreams and are always linked with an enumeration of my achievements and successes, as though I wanted to say: "You see, I have come to something."
>
> (Ibid., p. 215)

The dream ends with a scene in which the roles are "exchanged in revenge" (Ibid.): his father is humiliated, he is missing an eye – a reference to his glaucoma. In 1885, Freud's father had a surgery for glaucoma carried out by Dr Königstein, who was assisted by Koller and Freud himself. The associations between the two memories derived from Freud's dream show a tension between the two central aspects of his infantile oedipal ambition: to seduce his mother by becoming the great man she is hoping for, ready as she is to do anything to make her way in life; with his father, to turn humiliation into a triumph by demonstrating his creative powers, by succeeding where Joseph failed. Ambition is closely linked to erotised desires, from maternal seduction to the revenge against his father, which he tries to repair through tenderness, by wishing to buy him a new bed, red like the bathwater of his nursemaid.

These elements lead to a third series of ideas: the older man in Freud's dream is ultimately associated (in a note, p. 215) with "another interpretation": at first, his father is one-eyed like Odin, the father-god. Subsequently, Freud emphasises that he is mocking his father because he is blind, handing him a urinal; this reminds him of a story of a peasant who tries several different glasses at the optician's even though he cannot read, leading to a play on words which distinguishes between and connects the terms *Bauernländer* ("trickster") and *Mädchenfänger* ("womaniser"). Lastly, treating his father like a child reminds Freud of Zola's *La terre*, which tells the story of an old man, Fouan, whose three children abuse and eventually kill him once they have acquired his land.

We should note a first clue, which Freud does not identify: in the play on words, the association between unbridled sexuality and transgression, a recurrent theme in his work. In the fantasy, he can identify with the trickster-womaniser, echoing his self-description as a "scapegrace" in relation to the deflowering fantasies in the paper on the *Screen-Memories* (Freud, 1899, p. 315). And in German, another element slips in: the terms to describe youth or adolescence are basically the qualifiers *jung* or *Pubertät*, to which we could add the feminine *Mädchen*, which does not have a masculine equivalent. Both in his adolescent life and in his later work (Houssier, 2015; Houssier and Christaki, 2016), there was a constant preoccupation with young girls or young virgins – a link between his sexual fantasies and his interest in hysteria.

Let's return to Freud's commentary on these clusters of associations: "The tragic requital that lay in my father's soiling his bed like a child during the last days of his life; hence my appearance in the dream as a sick-nurse" (Freud, 1900, p. 216). This generational reversal – the child becomes the father's parent – obviously stems from a revenge for his childhood humiliation. Yet Freud highlights the fact that "Here it was as though thinking and experiencing were one and the same thing" (Ibid., original emphasis), which recalls "a strongly revolutionary literary play by Oskar Panizza ['Das Liebeskonzil' (1895)], in which God the Father is ignominiously treated as a paralytic old man" (Ibid.). This is how Freud concludes this long series of associations, which range from his childhood to his teenage years, without one taking priority over the other.

> My making plans was a reproach against my father dating from a later period. And indeed the whole rebellious content of the dream, with its lèse majesté and its derision of the higher authorities, went back to rebellion against my father.
>
> (Ibid.)

His emphasis on the image of a father tired and weakened by old age is connected to adolescence, a period where the symbolic murder may enlist the revolutionary tendencies fuelled by fantasy. In myths or literature we see parricide in its crudest, most primitive form, such as the story of Old Fouan, who can no longer protect himself from his children's evil designs. Jacob's destiny is taken over by Freud in his own revenge fantasies: reproaching Jacob for his weakness turns into a scenario of murdering the enfeebled father. In fine, there is yet another generational repetition. In her old age, Amalia kept her daughter Dolfi as her "staff of old age"; the same scenario was later replayed between Freud and his daughter Anna, who effectively became his "nurse".

2.6 Heroism and revenge

The death wishes against his father were part of the processes of de-idealisation caused by an experience of humiliation. In this context, the memory of Freud's father abused in the street by an anti-Semite has been most commented on. Freud's father would often take young Sigmund on walks in the forest, talking to him about his views upon the world. Here is the story as Freud reports it:

> Thus it was, on one such occasion, that he told me a story to show me how much better things were now than they had been in his days. "When I was a young man", he said, "I went for a walk one Saturday in the streets of your birthplace; I was well dressed, and had a new fur cap on my head. A Christian came up to me and with a single blow knocked off my cap into the mud and shouted: 'Jew! get off the pavement!'" "And what did you do?" I asked. "I went into the roadway and picked up my cap," was his quiet reply. This struck me as unheroic conduct on the part of the big, strong man who was holding the little boy by the hand.
>
> (Freud, 1900, p. 196)

The story of father's humiliation by an anti-Semite led to a daydream, a scene in which Hamilcar makes his son Hannibal swear he would take revenge against the Romans and defend Cartago to the death. The symbolic revalidation of the father by Hannibal's rebellion is in fact double-sided: in the heroic myth, the magnificent son surpasses the father, but also repairs the father's image, all the while changing his culture without ever betraying the Jewish identity of his ancestors (Roudinesco, 2014). Like Hannibal, Freud was an avenging conqueror.

Another memory, which is less well known, relates to his paternal uncle Josef Freud, who was arrested for possession of counterfeit bank notes and sentenced to ten years in prison. Freud experienced this event as a new humiliation of his father and remembered that, as a child, his relationship with his uncle was a source of both hatred and friendship (Roudinesco, 2014).

According to Breger (2000), public references to Freud's father present him as a strong and loving man, but they say nothing about his flaws – a source of shame, something to be hidden. While Sigmund presented himself as a precocious adolescent destined to achieve great things, Jacob slowly became more infantile and dependent on the help of others, which, to Freud's great distress, led to his family's impoverishment. His father seemed to be waiting for something to happen; in a letter to Martha, Freud looks at his father more tenderly, while also pointing out the mindset he reproaches him for: "When he isn't exactly grouchy, which alas is very often the case, he is the greatest optimist of all us young people" (1979, p. 22). Although it was often joked about, Jacob's lack of professional skills was a heavy burden on the entire family. Still, this did not prevent Freud from arguing that what a child needed was above all his father's protection (1930).

Freud compensated for the fragility of his father by identifying with various heroic historical figures. Krüll (1979) notes his enthusiasm for war heroes such as Hannibal, Napoleon, Alexander the Great and so on. Since childhood, his favourite character was the French military commander Masséna: he would stick little signs with the names of the empire's marshals on the backs of his toy soldiers. His preference for Masséna, whose name resembled that of the Jewish patriarch Manasseh, also had to do with their shared birthday. In the Bible, Mannaseh was an aggressive and bloodthirsty king, who came to the throne at only twelve years of age and later slashed his own son's throat and burnt his body in sacrifice – a figure that pandered to Freud's warlike ideal. This identification again returned during his self-analysis, after the death of his father.

At the age of ten, his passion for military characters merged with nationalist sentiments; he skipped school in order to make bandages for the veterans of the Austro-Prussian war, which shook the entire Franz Joseph's monarchy (Schur, 1972). Krüll associates Freud's military fantasies with his ambivalence towards John: he argues that the identification with the victorious warriors was a fulfilment of the wish to win and triumph over his nephew, while usually he was dominated by him. Once again, the figure of the frenemy and the father come together. Note that one of his most common mistakes in *The Interpretation of Dreams* is to confuse the name of his hero, Hamilcar: he replaces the father's name with that of the brother during three subsequent proof corrections (1900, p. 196, note1). As we shall see in the scene between Caesar and Brutus, the mixture of fratricidal and patricidal wishes is prominent here.

The historical figures he identified with also show that reading was essential to him already as a child, before it became a genuine passion in adolescence and an endless source of personal growth. "One of the first books that I got hold of when I had learnt to read was Thiers' history of the Consulate and Empire", he remembers (Ibid.). This is where he found the names of the Empire's marshals. Both his longing for a heroic father and his ideas about romantic love came from books.

When it comes to the writing of Freud's own heroic story of his descent into the depths of the human soul, his biographers have highlighted a certain psychoanalytical myth of origins: Freud as the solitary and courageous hero bravely defying the social mores of his time. This kind of romance suggests the hero's complete originality with respect to his predecessors, peers, disciples or rivals. The same idea echoes in Freud's words to Silberstein, when he writes that "the eternal glory of the idea will be linked with my name" – regardless of the use made of it by other scientists, he adds with a degree of enthusiasm bordering on megalomania (Freud, 1871–1881, p. 33). Seducing his mother, becoming a hero like Oedipus, as well as freeing himself from her would all depend on his professional success, which would also allow him to surpass his father.

2.7 The passion for books

The importance of the father-son bond, also one of the guiding threats of Freud's work (Houssier, 2013a), is illustrated by the following anecdote. In 1891, Jacob gifted his son with a Bible, in which he wrote the following dedication:

My dear Son,
    It was in the seventh year of your age that the spirit of God began to move you to learning. I would say the spirit of God speaketh to you: "Read in My book; there will be opened to thee sources of knowledge and of the intellect." It is the Book of Books; it is the well that wise men have digged and from which lawgivers have drawn the waters of their knowledge.
    Thou hast seen in this Book the vision of the Almighty, thou hast heard willingly, thou hast done and hast tried to fly high upon the wings of the Holy Spirit. Since then I have preserved the same Bible. Now, on your thirty-fifth birthday, I have brought it out from its retirement and I send it to you as a token of love from your old father (Schur, 1972, p. 24).

In the Bible, Jacob also wrote down, in Hebrew, the date of his father's death.
    Several years before his death on 23rd October 1896, Freud's father expressed his affection in terms of a transmission and highlighted the sacred nature of books. Freud (1925) remembers that he started reading the Bible shortly after learning how to read and that it had a decisive influence on his future interests.
    For Huber (2009), Freud's love of books was linked to his father's passion for the Torah and biblical history. This is his interpretation of the gift of the sacred book: "Father tells son: read this book, which must be read because it unknown,

or rather: read the unknown to be found in this well-known book" (Huber, 2009, p. 91). This implicit injunction oriented Freud's drive for knowledge, encouraging him to take the lead in a new transmission. Following along the lines of "Golden Sigi", Jacob imagined his son had a divine essence. He compared him to God and believed that Sigmund was going to bring something new to Judaism. Jacob's friend Samuel Hammerschlag became Sigmund's religion teacher and later a kind of paternal confidant. In a letter to Martha from 10th January 1884, Freud pays tribute to him, praising "the deep-seated sympathy which has existed between myself and the dear old Jewish teacher ever since my school days" (1873–1939, p. 86). Hammerschlag was among the generous donors or lenders to repeatedly help Freud financially; he is described as one of the kindest and most humane people Freud knew, "further removed from any ignoble motives", who taught Sigismund to overcome the miseries of everyday life by immersing himself in literature.

One of his earliest memories again connects Freud to his father and to books. After the dream of the botanical manuscript (Freud, 1900), considered among the most significant fantasies of his adolescence, he remembers that his father gave him and his sister Anna a book from which they could pull the pages out leaf by leaf. The flower which the dream designates as his favourite – the artichoke – connects the dream to his fantasies. He writes: "Behind 'artichokes' lay, on the one hand, my thoughts about Italy and, on the other hand, a scene from my childhood which was the opening of what have since become my intimate relations with books" (Freud, 1900, p. 282). This relation can be traced to a seemingly everyday scene, which is nevertheless connected to his father's ideas about child-rearing or indeed a kind of paternal authorisation for the child to exercise his destructive powers.

> There followed, I could not quite make out how, a recollection from very early youth. It had once amused my father to hand over a book with coloured plates (an account of a journey through Persia) for me and my eldest sister to destroy. Not easy to justify from the educational point of view! I had been five years old at the time and my sister not yet three; and the picture of the two of us blissfully pulling the book to pieces (leaf by leaf, like an artichoke, I found myself saying) was almost the only plastic memory that I retained from that period of my life.
>
> (Ibid., p. 171)

He then makes a connection with his student days:

> Then, when I became a student, I had developed a passion for collecting and owning books, which was analogous to my liking for learning out of monographs: a favourite hobby, (The idea of "favourite" had already appeared in connection with cyclamens and artichokes.) I had become a book-worm (cf. herbarium). I had always, from the time I first began to think about

myself, referred this first passion of mine back to the childhood memory I have mentioned. Or rather, I had recognized that the childhood scene was a "screen memory" for my later bibliophile propensities.

(Ibid., p. 171–172)

The relationship established here between his childhood memory and his student life is silent on the bibliophile tendencies, which started long before his university years, as attested to by the abundance of literary references in his correspondence with Silberstein (Freud, 1871–1881). Another key biographical element appears, this time through a memory of Freud's brother Alexander. When Sigmund was ten, his parents asked him what he thought they should name his youngest brother and, given his passion for historical characters, he suggested "Alexander" and his parents accepted. Six years later, Sigmund said to his brother: "Look Alexander, our family is like a book. You are the youngest and I the oldest, and so we are like two solid lids that support and protect the weak sisters born after me and before you" (Eissler, 2006, p. 59). We could dwell on the clichés of the weak woman and the strong and protective man, and glimpse a potential masochistic tendency here; but instead, let's focus on the protective and containing aspects of his idea of the two poles of the sibling group, in the clearly somewhat enclosed family universe. The two brothers represent the two lids of a box containing the fragile sisters, who are sheltered but also surrounded by the two sentries – substitutes for the absent or lacking paternal figures. The allusion to books is also interesting: following his interests, the metaphor which came to his mind when speaking to his brother transforms the book into a kind of envelope which, like a mother's arms wrapped around her baby, takes care of the entire family universe.

The absence of parental references is also indicative of Freud's role as his family's spokesperson and of the responsibilities given to him as the eldest son, as if he was in a position to lead the whole family. This is obvious in the story of the choice of his brother's name.

Another moment of his life corroborates this impression. Sigmund's sister Anna was the family's only daughter to study and become a teacher. Freud was horrified by the marriage proposal made to his then sixteen-year-old sister by an elderly uncle from the mother's family, the Nathansons. As an eighteen-year-old, he felt strongly opposed to it. Eventually, Anna married Martha Bernays' brother Eli and they moved to the United States, where they had five children together (Bernays, 1940). Sigmund's parents treated their son as an authority, allowing him to intervene in the family in sometimes a puritanical and censoring manner, on matters such as his brother's schoolwork or his sister Anna's reading choices, where he considered Balzac not to be a suitable author for a girl of fifteen (Gay, 1991).

Bibliography

Abraham R. (1982), Freud's mother and the formulation of the oedipal father, *The Psychoanalytic Review*, 69, p. 441–453.

Bernays A. (1940), My brother Sigmund Freud, *American Mercury*, LI, p. 335–342.

Bernfeld S. (1922, 1995), Concerning a typical form of male puberty, *Adolescent psychiatry*, 22, p. 51–66.

Bernfeld S. (1944), Freud's early childhood, *Bulletin of the Menninger Clinic*, 8, p. 105–115.

Breger L. (2000), *Freud: Darkness in the Midst of Vision*, New York, Wiley.

Eissler K. R. (1978), Creativity and adolescence: the effect of trauma in Freud's adolescence, *The Psychoanalytic Study of the Child*, 33, p. 461–518.

Eissler K. R. (2006), Esquisse biographique, in Eissler K., Freud E., Freud L., Grubitch Simitis I., Fleckhaus W. (dir.), *Sigmund Freud. Lieux, visages, objets*, Paris, Gallimard, p. 10–38.

Freud M. (1958), *Sigmund Freud: Man and Father*, New York, Vanguard Press.

Freud S. (1871–1881, 1990), *Lettres de jeunesse*, Paris, Gallimard.

Freud S. (1899), *Screen Memories*. SE 3, London, Hogarth Press, p. 299–322.

Freud S. (ed.). (1900), *The Interpretation of Dreams*. SE 4, London, Hogarth Press, p. ix–627.

Freud S. (1905), *Fragment of an Analysis of a Case of Hysteria (1905 [1901])*. SE 7, London, Hogarth Press, p. 1–122.

Freud S. (1910–1918), *Contributions to the Psychology of Love*. SE 11, London, Hogarth Press, p. 163–208.

Freud S. (1917, 1933), Un souvenir d'enfance dans "Fiction et vérité" de Goethe, in *Essais de psychanalyse appliquée*, Paris, Gallimard, p. 149–162.

Freud S. (1925), *An Autobiographical Study*. SE 20, London, Hogarth Press, p. 1–70.

Freud S. (1930), *Civilization and its Discontents*. SE 21, London, Hogarth Press, p. 57–146.

Freud S. (1931a), *Letter from Sigmund Freud to The Mayor of Příbor-Freiberg, October 25, 1931*. Letters of Sigmund Freud 1873–1939 51, London, Hogarth Press, p. 407–408.

Freud S. (1931b), *Female Sexuality*. SE 21, London, Hogarth Press, p. 221–244.

Freud S. (1933), *New Introductory Lectures on Psycho-Analysis*. SE 22, London, Hogarth Press, p. 1–182.

Freud S. (1935), *An Autobiographical Study*. SE 20, London, Hogarth Press, p. 71–74.

Freud S. (1936), *A Disturbance of Memory on the Acropolis*. SE 22, London, Hogarth Press, p. 237–248.

Freud S. (1979), *Correspondance (1873–1939)*, Paris, Gallimard.

Freud S. (1986), *The Complete Letters to Wilhelm Fliess (1887–1904)*, Cambridge, MA, Harvard University Press.

Freud S., Breuer J. (1895), *Studies on Hysteria*. SE 2, London, Hogarth Press, p. ix–310.

Gay P. (1988, 1991), *Freud: A Life for Our Time*, New York, W.W. Norton & Co.

Hardin H. T. (1987), On the vicissitudes of Freud's early mothering: I. early environment and loss, *Psychoanalytic Quarterly*, 56, p. 628–644.

Heim S. (1990), Note préliminaire, in Freud S. (ed.), *Lettres de jeunesse*, Paris, Gallimard, p. 7–8.

Houssier F. (2010), *L'école d'Anna Freud. Créativité et controverses*, Paris, Editions Campagne Première.

Houssier F. (2013a), *Meurtres dans la famille*, Paris, Dunod.

Houssier F. (2013b), L'adolescent, ce visiteur de l'archaïque (El adolescente, este visitante de lo arcaico), in Controversias on Line. *Psicoanalisis de ninos y adolescentes* (APdeBA), 12, p. 58–71.

Houssier F. (2013c), Sigmund Freud/Eduard Silberstein: une amitié passionnelle et con-sanguine, *Adolescence*, 83, 31(1), p. 219–226.

Houssier F. (2015), Freud adolescent, in Perron R., Missonnier S. (dir.), *Les Cahiers de l'Herne*, Freud, Paris, Flammarion, p. 31–37.

Houssier F. (2016), Entre S. Freud et S. Ferenczi, un Œdipe pubertaire?, *Les lettres de la SPF*, 35, p. 157–173.

Houssier F., Christaki A. (2016), Folie pubertaire et sexualité diabolique dans les débuts de la psychanalyse, *Topique*, 134, p. 157–170.

Huber G. (2009), *Si c'était Freud*, Lormond, Le bord de l'eau.

Krüll M. (1979), *Sigmund, fils de Jacob*, Paris, Gallimard.

Panizza O. (1895, 2017), *Das Liebeskonzil*, Hofenberg.

Roudinesco E. (2014, 2016), *Freud: In His Time and Ours*, Cambridge, MA, Harvard University Press.

Schur M. (1972), *Freud: Living and Dying*, Cambridge, International University Press.

Ticho E., Ticho G. (1972), Freud and the Viennese, *The International Journal of Psychoa-nalysis*, 53, p. 301–306.

Chapter 3

Adolescent life

Freud's adolescence was a time of waiting, for a grandiose destiny that would make his mother's hopes come true. After the family's move in 1875, Sigmund was the only one of their six children to have his own room, a long and narrow "office" where he would sleep, study and often eat alone while reading. He studied late into the night under a shabby oil lamp and felt embarrassed for not owning a dictionary. His studies were his parents' only extraordinary expenditure.

It is also in his academic life that the traces of his adolescence emerge most strongly, highlighting the conflict between submission and rebellion against authority.

3.1 An (almost) model student

Freud started at the Leopoldstadter Real und Obergymnasium a year early, quite in line with his fantasies of intellectual superiority. Prior to middle school, his main source of knowledge had been his father, who transmitted to him a desire for learning and a sense of discipline key to academic success. However, in her memoir, his sister Anna writes that it was their mother who had been first in charge of Freud's learning and gave him lessons at home (Krüll, 1979, p. 340) before his father took over. In any case, Freud started at the Leopoldstadt Secondary Municipal School for Arts and Sciences in September 1865. At the time, Vienna had only four secondary schools, of which two were faith schools, before the government took over all academic institutions in 1869. Freud's middle and secondary school was founded in 1864 and built up until 1872; its objective was to impart higher general education with a focus on classical languages such as Latin, Greek or French, as well as sciences, in order to prepare students for university. During the first two years before Freud's *Matura* (the final examination), two hours weekly were devoted to "Philosophical Propaedeutics", which included logic and psychology. The teaching staff comprised a number of personalities distinguished in their respective fields: the Principal Dr Abis Pokorny was a botanist and zoologist; he appears in Freud's dream of the botanical monograph as a rather severe figure, distrustful of young Sigmund. The faculty also included Hammerschlag, who taught religion two hours per week. Dr Viktor von Kraus, the history teacher,

DOI: 10.4324/9781003340898-3

is associated with the dream of the one-eyed doctor. These teachers also regularly lectured at the university (Knöpfmacher, 1979).

Eissler writes about Freud's middle-school beginnings: "It often happened that the most gifted pupils were exposed, due to their very talent, to situations where they had to compete with physically far more mature students. This is what happened to Freud" (1974, p. 69). For a long time, he had much older friends, as attested by the programme of a school celebration in honour of Schiller, on 11th November 1868. Young Freud recited *The Ring of Polycrates* and then also played Margot in the prologue to the *Virgin of Orleans*, alongside a first-year female student in the role of Johanna. A year nine student, he was twelve years old at the time. Eissler believes that he was given a female role because his voice had not yet changed; he had not started puberty. The fourteen- and fifteen-year-olds in his class were likely to be more mature physically.

> If we now consider that the onset of physical maturity comes especially late for those who are the most gifted, we can assume that, for many years, Freud had been subject to extreme tension, because in terms of physical maturity he was one of the last ones in his class and his classmates were all physically ahead of him,

Eissler argues (Ibid.). He also points out (1978) that throughout his life, Freud complained about his intellectual failings, a feeling Eissler relates to his reported sense of lagging behind in terms of physical maturity. He supports his hypothesis by noting that for years Freud suffered from the anxiety of missing the train – as if he imagined he would never grow up; his extreme ambition thus betrayed a sense of impatience in waiting to reach maturity.

During the eight years of secondary school, until the age of seventeen, he was nearly always at the top of his class (Gicklhorn, 1965). Nonetheless, there were several incidents of failure, as we learn from his associations with the dream of the botanical monograph:

> I will make an attempt at interpreting the other determinants of the content of the dream as well. There was a dried specimen of the plant included in the monograph, as though it had been a herbarium. This led me to a memory from my secondary school. Our headmaster once called together the boys from the higher forms and handed over the school's herbarium to them to be looked through and cleaned.
>
> (Freud, 1900, p. 170)

He adds that the headmaster did not seem to have much confidence in him and only gave him a few sheets to clean. He goes on:

> In my preliminary examination in botany I was also given a Crucifer to identify – and failed to do so. My prospects would not have been too bright,

if I had not been helped out by my theoretical knowledge. I went on from the Cruciferae to the Compositae. It occurred to me that artichokes were Compositae, and indeed I might fairly have called them my *favourite flowers*.

(Ibid.)

In this memory, theoretical knowledge from books is a solution to a situation that sets up a fantasy of castration via the figure of the severe headmaster.

3.2 Giving one's life to a greater cause

Consistent with his mother's desire, Freud also had a privileged position in his class and almost never had to sit exams. However, moving on to secondary school, there were two distinct periods: at first, he presented himself as a rebel, which he mentions in a letter to Martha.

One would hardly guess it from looking at me, and yet even at school I was always the bold oppositionist, always on hand when an extreme had to be defended and usually ready to atone for it. As I moved up into the favoured position of head boy, where I remained for years and was generally trusted, people no longer had any reason to complain about me,

(Freud, 1873–1939, p. 201)

he writes, as if to suggest that only the fact of being first in his class and the certainty of being loved quelled his desire to rebel. The two last memories share a common theme, namely the need to be trusted by a supportive adult. Trust and later mistrust were also to be a theme in Freud's subsequent friendships, for example with Wilhelm Fliess.

An anecdote substantiates Freud's assertion of his rebellious tendencies: at thirteen, he stood in solidarity with two classmates. An inquiry led by the history professor Hannak found out that for several months the duo had been touring the taverns of Leopoldstadt and Wieden, playing pool and visiting prostitutes. Together with his friend Heinrich Braun, who taught him to look at the world critically and instilled in him certain revolutionary ideas, Freud knew about the situation but kept quiet until the secret was revealed, and he too was questioned. Together with another classmate, Gustav Altzinger, he remained silent as the two wrongdoers were expelled, but subsequently his "conduct mark" dropped for a failure to report (Eissler, 2006). Looking at Freud's report cards, Renée Gicklhorn tells us that while his conduct was normally always "perfect", in the 1870–1871 school year it was reduced to "fair" for the entire class. The teachers' report for Freud's class of 1869, which Gicklhorn was able to find, says that three year nine students had showed unruly behaviour in class, and outside the school had mingled with "debauched" women. She notes that Freud's attitude changed when he was made the head boy, like a war hero, an assertive and ambitious leader; he became a "deserving student" according to the then-applicable school notation and was very often the best in his class. In the Germanic grading system of the time, where "1" stood for excellent and "6" for insufficient, he regularly obtained 1.5.

He explains his revolutionary tendencies to Martha. "I have often felt as though I had inherited all the defiance and all the passions with which our ancestors defended their Temple and could gladly sacrifice my life for one great moment in history" (Freud, 1873–1939, p. 201), he writes, identifying with the Jewish heroes of the past generations. Freud's friends at school were also only Jewish boys, despite his class including a number of Catholics (Boehlich, 1990).

Another scene emerges from the dream of Count Thun, showing that when it came to defending certain ideas, Freud was indeed fearless:

> The insolent attitude adopted by the Count in the dream was copied from a scene at my secondary school when I was fifteen years old. We had hatched a conspiracy against an unpopular and ignorant master, the moving spirit of which had been one of my schoolfellows who since those days seemed to have taken Henry VIII of England as his model. The leadership in the chief assault was allotted to me, and the signal for open revolt was a discussion on the significance of the Danube to Austria (cf. the Wachau). One of our fellow-conspirators had been the only aristocratic boy in the class, who, on account of his remarkable length of limb, was called "the Giraffe". He was standing up, like the Count in my dream, having been taken to task by the school tyrant, the German language master.
>
> (Freud, 1900, p. 210–211)

In adolescence, the figures of Masséna and Hannibal he had looked up to as a child became part of his ego ideal, like the revolutionary spirit expressed in these early years and again later in his dreams. This time, Hannibal is mentioned in relation to Freud's adolescence:

> I had actually been following in Hannibal's footsteps. Like him, I had been fated not to see Rome; and he too had moved into the Campagna when everyone had expected him in Rome. But Hannibal, whom I had come to resemble in these respects, had been the favourite hero of my later school days. Like so many boys of that age, I had sympathized in the Punic Wars not with the Romans but with the Carthaginians. And when in the higher classes I began to understand for the first time what it meant to belong to an alien race, and anti-Semitic feelings among the other boys warned me that I must take up a definite position, the figure of the Semitic general rose still higher in my esteem. To my youthful mind Hannibal and Rome symbolized the conflict between the tenacity of Jewry and the organization of the Catholic church. And the increasing importance of the effects of the anti-Semitic movement upon our emotional life helped to fix the thoughts and feelings of those early days.
>
> (Freud, 1900, p. 195)

Gedo and Wolf (1976) point out that this identification is linked to his father's humiliation by the anti-Semite, while Jones (1958) understands Freud's admiration for Hannibal as a symbol of refusing submission and instead ultimately becoming the winner. And yet, Hannibal eventually failed to defeat Scipio Africanus, who avenged his father's humiliation in the battles against the Carthaginians at Ticinus and the Trebia.

Later at university, in one of his letters to Silberstein, Freud relates another significant episode from his school years. Having described the balmy air of the dissection hall, he talks about the charged atmosphere in which law students and teachers were criticised and called to order by the Minister of Education. The new university rector Dr Wahlberg denounced these threats to academic freedoms in his speech at a large demonstration. Freud's delight is palpable, evoking his taste for rebellions that contest power and authority, recalled in his later text on schoolboy psychology (Freud, 1914b). Written in a journalistic tone, his letter concludes with a note of admiration for the audacity and truth of the speech admonishing the current government (Freud, 1871–1881, p. 64–66).

These revolutionary ideas continued to gain ground. In his letter from 1883, he tells Martha that he is obsessed with his family's and especially his siblings' continuous subjection to poverty. He feels guilty for not being able to give anything up; when he thinks of them, he is upset and full of remorse. Seeing children running to their wet nurse, he thinks of his sister Marie, or "Mitzi", who in the meantime has become a governess, and grows "very, very furious and full of revolutionary thoughts" (Freud, 1873–1939, p. 172). In another letter to his fiancée, he writes that one evening Breuer told him something very touching, namely that under his timidity, he saw him as someone extremely daring and fearless, which Freud had always felt but never dared to express. Nevertheless, he has felt helpless, unable to translate his ardent passions into words or poems. "So I have always restrained myself, and it is this, I think, which people must see in me" (Ibid., p. 203), he writes, painting a picture of himself, as Elisabeth Roudinesco puts it, as a "well-governed rebel" (2016, p. 20).

In several of his later essays, Freud displayed keen social and political sensibility, for example in his wish to use child analysis as a preventative measure against neurosis. This shows that throughout his life, he largely remained faithful to the revolutionary ideals of his youth and to the painful experience of poverty. He points out the need to change the social order generated by capitalist dominance, criticising the rich who can satisfy their desires at will, a catalyst for a social protest against such privilege (Freud, 1905b).

3.3 Meeting a young professor

In middle school and later in secondary school, Freud took Latin, which he had begun studying at the age of nine. He read Livy's *The History of Rome*, where he discovered the story of Hannibal but also Ovid's *Metamorphoses* and their incorporations of Greek myths; plus, Cicero and, in 1873, Horace's *The Odes*, mentioned in his obituary of Karl Abraham (Freud, 1926). Demosthenes,

Sophocles, Homer's *Iliad*, Xenophon, the Greco-Persian wars and Plato were also among his literary journeys. He was familiar with Virgil and repeatedly cites from the *Aeneid* in some of the earliest publications on psychoanalysis (1900, 1901).

He considers the essay on *Nature* misattributed to Goethe[1] as a turning point; reading it several months before his sixteenth birthday changed his destiny and Goethe became one of his teenage hero identifications. His love of nature led him to read botanical monographies, develop an interest in *osteology* or the transformation of one's inner being based on *Poetry and Truth* by Goethe, with whom he shared these areas of interest. He later based his analysis of Goethe's childhood memories on the same text (Freud, 1917).

From his reading as a schoolboy, Freud drew everything he loved about the Greek and Roman cultures, especially his passion for sculpture and archaeology. In his work, the psychoanalytic concepts of Eros and Thanatos, narcissism and the Oedipus complex, to only mention a few, show that these classical myths indeed left an indelible mark (Trosman, 1978). Darwin's theories were also part of the curriculum. All these cultural and identity references were of great interest to young Freud and stayed in his memory throughout his life, akin to a crucible waiting to be reclaimed by psychoanalytic theory.

On the occasion of the school's 50th anniversary, Freud was asked to write a contribution (Freud, 1914b). This provoked different feelings in him: he felt ready to obey like a soldier and was surprised by how quickly he had said yes. However, his sense of puzzlement went further. While about to turn sixty at the time of this request, he remembered having once met one of his teachers on the street and thinking:

> How youthful he looks! And how old you yourself have grown! How old can he be to-day? Can it be possible that the men who used to stand for us as types of adulthood were really so little older than we were?
>
> (Freud, 1914b, p. 240)

This triggered a fantasy of a generational difference too narrow not to trouble Freud, who was himself now called "Professor" by his psychoanalytic students.

To Silberstein, Freud spoke about their situation as young men, still living with their families but also on the cusp of leaving home. In his text on the suicides of secondary-school pupils, his position is fairly critical:

> But a secondary school should achieve more than not driving its pupils to suicide. It should give them a desire to live and should offer them support and backing at a time of life at which the conditions of their development compel them to relax their ties with their parental home and their family. It seems to me indisputable that schools fail in this, and in many respects fall short of their duty of providing a substitute for the family and of arousing interest in life in the world outside.
>
> (Freud, 1910, p. 231–232)

Despite having made a place for himself at his own school, his words echo a sense of lack of support in shaking off the heavy burden of his family, as he also stresses in his letter to Rolland, where he recalls his desire to flee the suffocating atmosphere of the family universe.

His critical attitude towards his secondary school extended to student-teacher relationships; teachers were loved and hated in equal measure, which somewhat takes away from the idea of blindly following orders, or even of standing at attention, unless we see this as a binary opposition between submission and rebellion. Nevertheless, he adds:

> At such moments as these, I used to find, the present time seemed to sink into obscurity and the years between ten and eighteen would rise from the corners of my memory, with all their guesses and illusions, their painful distortions and heartening successes – my first glimpses of an extinct civilization (which in my case was to bring me as much consolation as anything else in the struggles of life), my first contacts with the sciences, among which it seemed open to me to choose to which of them I should dedicate what were no doubt my inestimable services.
>
> (Freud, 1914c, p. 241)

These memories of adolescence, attesting to the intensity of the tensions felt at the time, are combined with a sense of a mandate, a mission to accomplish. He continues, in a prophetic tone:

> And I seem to remember that through the whole of this time there ran a premonition of a task ahead, till it found open expression in my school-leaving essay as a wish that I might during the course of my life contribute something to our human knowledge.
>
> (Ibid., p. 242)

3.4 The birth of a hero

At the age of thirteen, a year which seems the most silent in the life of young Freud (Rodrigué, 2000), and during the first four years of secondary school, until 1869, Freud was enrolled as "Sigismund". Starting from his fifth year, in 1870, he changed his given name to the more classical "Sigmund". In his correspondence with Silberstein, he signed off as Sigmund for the first time in September 1872, without completely giving up Sigismund, which still appeared several times over the following two years.

In these letters, he also used diminutives such as "Sig", attesting to his search for an identity as a young man, until the fantasy of self-engendering took over and he changed his given name, thus distancing himself from his Jewish origins. Anzieu situates the moment of Freud's definitive abandonment of his childhood name between 1877 and 1878, linked to his first scientific publications. However, a different hypothesis emerges from the letters to Silberstein: in April 1875, the signature "Sigismund" appears for the last time and "Sigmund", already present in 1872 in Freud's letters to Emil Fluss, is kept until the end of their correspondence. If we think of adolescence as a painful process of transformation, Freud changed one of the most precise components of his sense of identity, his given name – a sign of a desire to re-create himself. This desire, underpinned by a fantasy of self-creation, helped fuel his self-image as a hero defying the theories of his day and bringing about an intellectual revolution ex-nihilo. This fantasy, the limits of which we know today, was fundamentally bisexual, in that Freud both fecundates and gives birth to the psychoanalytic theory.

This myth of the hero scientist, largely supported by Jones' "official" biography (1958) – a work not without merit – paints a picture of Freud struggling alone against anti-Semitism, the hostility of the academic world or Victorian morality. His desire to make up for the image of the fallen father by following his oedipal desire by becoming, against the backdrop of his mother's social redemption, the heroic son involves a series of revenge fantasies, the source of which is condensed in the episode of the anti-Semite's attack on father.

The theme of the struggle against anti-Semitism returns in a scene where young Freud is ready to throw a punch to defend his honour and the figure of his father. As a student, he became the target of anti-Semitic slurs while travelling by train and got up to fight the two or three men who had provoked him (Rodrigué, 2000). He then wrote to Martha that only a year earlier he would have been paralysed by anger, but since they had met, he had changed: this kind of mob no longer scares him and he feels ready for a fight (Freud, 1873–1939, p. 78).

When he proudly announces to Martha his auto-da-fé, in which he destroyed all that he had written as a young boy, including his notes and probably his journal, he calls this "The Development of the Hero" (Ibid., p. 141) and speaks about himself in the third person. This perception of his youth shows the persistence of a childhood fantasy centred on the mythical construction of a hero. Like Hannibal, Freud felt himself to be a "conquistador by temperament", as he wrote to Silberstein, an expression later used in a letter to Ferenczi.

To put this more clearly, if the first "official" biography penned by Jones largely contributed to maintaining Freud's image as an absolute hero, the creator of psychoanalysis, Freud himself played a role in creating this story of origins. In his work, the primal horde has to create a new myth of origins, the origins of humanity. This transfer of the theme into Freud's work required a certain depersonalisation, yet its biographical sources are fairly obvious. Adolescence initially strengthened and potentiated Freud's teenage fantasies of omnipotence, which helped him imagine his own narcissistic history. In short, Freud's own history and the genesis of psychoanalysis are inextricably linked; they share a number of pubertal fantasies (Gutton, 1996), including the fantasy of self-engendering and of creating one's own legend.

3.5 A young monk discovers free-association

Freud's thirteenth year was marked by two works, one because of its closeness to his fantasies, the other because it indicates the crucial influence of some of his teenage experiences on the rest of his life and career. Freud remembers the first book, the 1853 novel *Hypatia*, by Charles Kingsley, in connection with the dream of the "Three Fates". The hero of the story, a young monk named Philammon, struggles against incestual desires for his sister.

> I have never known the name of the novel or of its author; but I have a vivid memory of its ending. The hero went mad and kept calling out the names of the three women who had brought the greatest happiness and sorrow into his life.
>
> (Freud, 1900, p. 204)

Some thirty years later, Freud's earnestness sheds light on what truly counted for him as an adolescent: incestual desires not just for his mother but also his sister. He later returned to this theme in his work, stressing the need to surmount the incestuous fixations to both figures (1910–1918, p. 179). However, also and more specifically linked the adolescent psyche, it concern the frightening intensity of these desires – a fear of madness that might well be among the most frequent fantasies of adolescence. In this perspective, note that Freud also identified the fantasy of being Christ as typical of adolescence (Freud, 1908). This echoes his own identification with the crucified Christ in a letter to Fliess on 23rd March 1900, where he describes his current depressive episode: "No one can help me in the least with what oppresses me; it is my cross, I must bear it; and God knows that in adapting to it, my back has become noticeably bent" (Freud, 1887–1904, p. 406). He would also combine religion and intimate relationships by calling Fliess "Daimonie" or his little daughter Anna the "black devil", long before she became "Antigone" (Houssier, 2010).

His identification with the monk Philammon reappears in some of his letters to Silberstein and to his fiancée; in a first letter from 1883, he complains to Martha about their long separation, after she has moved near Hamburg with her family: "Continually having so much to do acts as a kind of narcotic", he writes, looking for something to help him overcome his highly emotional and excitable state. Like the protagonist of *Ekkehard*, a romance by Joseph Victor von Scheffel, he is at times tempted by "the waves of the great world", at other times forced to "fight against the sensation of being a monk in his cell" (Freud, 1873–1939, p. 67). Von Scheffel also penned a poem about the Cretaceans, which in a letter to Silberstein led Freud to nickname his love interest *Ichthyosaura* (1871–1881, p. 5).

He returns to the fantasy of monastic life later in the same letter: he writes that whenever a letter is coming from his fiancée, "the whole dream fades, life enters my cell" (Freud, 1873-1939, p. 67). At those moments, not just problems seem to fade away but also his passion for medicine. It is much lovelier to be a human being than a warehouse for certain monotonous experiences. This monastic life is a legacy of boyhood largely spent reading and daydreaming, without any sexual contact with girls. And although at this time Freud had already chosen his career path and was working like a madman to succeed, it is no coincidence that monastic life and its pull towards essentially incestuous fantasies (Freud, 1905a) was a convincing metaphor of young Freud's inner life.

Another religious element should be mentioned here; Huber (2009) argues that in a discussion about Sigmund's bar-mitsvah, the thirteen-year-old boy said he was opposed to it and Jacob, accepting his son's decision, gave him a book by Ludwig Börne. Börne's essay *How to Become an Original Writer in Three Days*, published in 1823, was an exploration of irony, incidental thoughts, free association and ways of overcoming self-censorship. At fifteen, Freud was inspired by it to write several aphorisms, five of which were subsequently published in the school magazine (Eissler, 2006). Aichhorn highlights the interest of this publication, *Musarion*, one of the few rare documents spared by Freud's auto-da-fé. The handwritten issue features *Snowdrop*, a poem by Fleischer, an obituary of the historian and politician Georg Gottfriend Gervinus (1805–1871), as well as *Memory and Hope* and a commentary on Goethe's *Singer*, both by Fleischer, and finally *Random Thoughts* by Sigmund Freud. Here are some of Freud's associative thoughts (Aichhorn, 2014, p. 623):

Gold inflates man like air a hog's bladder.
The most selfish of all is the man who has never thought of himself as such.
Some people are like a rich mine that has never been fully explored.
Others take stock of their thoughts like their laundry; they stab every little
  worm that gets lost in the wasteland of their brain.
Some people are ores, others are fool's gold, they only shine on the surface.
Any large animal outdoes a man in some way; but he outdoes them in every
way.

It seems difficult to interpret this kind of material, but we can nevertheless identify a few associative tracks which might help us understand the inner life of its young author. The first aphorism evokes the poverty of Freud's home. Eissler argues that because of his family's money woes, Freud intended to go work in the gold trade. His interest in ores, specifically gold, in fact reminds us of his mother's nickname, "Golden Sigi", and seems associated with his own self-perception projected into these lines; the inflated man conjures up certain megalomaniac fantasies, while the rich and underexplored mine seems a sort of self-definition.

We also see Freud's passion for observing human beings, distinguishing between the selfish, who only sparkle superficially, and those with more substance, akin to the more discreet but profound minerals. In this sense, Eissler points out that throughout his life, Freud remained wary of his lack of discernment and even of his intelligence, which he considered hardly average, while at the same time idealising it as an essential value, for himself and in his relationships with others.

3.6 A gift for life

Börne was a German Jew, a physician by training and an admirer of the French revolution, born on the same date, exactly a hundred years before Freud. The latter remembered the following sentence from the book, which he still kept in his library fifty years later: "A shameful and cowardly fear of thinking holds every one of us back" (Roudinesco, 2016, p. 18). In a letter to Ferenczi from 1919, Freud returns to this precious volume:

> I received Börne very early as a present, perhaps for my 13th birthday, read him with great enthusiasm, always had a strong recollection of some of these little essays. Naturally not the one on cryptomnesia. When I reread it, I was astonished at how much some things that are in there correspond almost word for word with some things that I have always represented and thought. So he could really be the source of my originality.
>
> (Freud, 1914–1919, p. 344)

On examining his cryptomnesia, he suggests that forgetting the influences of one's youth reveals a tendency to dismiss the contributions of the older generations against whom one is struggling (Trosman, 1969, p. 494). This parricidal fantasy of freeing oneself from the burden of tradition and the past is linked to the idea that the originality of many new thoughts evaporates in the untraceability and indetermination of repression.

Even while working in the scientific lab, Freud kept Börne's book in his library, which Trosman sees as a sign of keeping his faith in his intrapsychic process. He points out that Freud also visited Börne's grave in Paris, as if this meant crossing the boundary between organic medicine and his attraction for psychology. Börne's book and his ideas arrived at a moment when his youthful creativity was suffused by an intense feeling of his own uniqueness, as evidenced by his correspondence with Silberstein.

Trosman (1978) points to another key aspect of the future creator of psychoanalysis. In his work on how to become an original writer, Börne suggested that one should write down everything that came to one's mind, whether it had to do with oneself, one's wife, superiors and so on. Freud himself indicated (1920, 1937) that his rediscovery of Börne's essay helped him understand that in many cases, apparent originality concealed such cryptomnesic fragments. His rereading of it suggests that his memories of adolescence would repeatedly resurface, showing that as part of his "permanent" self-analysis, his adolescent experience remained alive within him.

Trosman nevertheless makes a more specific argument, namely that the reference to Börne as the source of the free-associative method was repudiated rather than simply forgotten. His hypothesis implies that some parts of Freud's adolescence underwent massive repression; that this discovery, which openly undermines the hero myth, dates back to the age of thirteen or fourteen; that its repression stems from its association with certain incestual fantasies and manifests specifically by taking on the mask of ironic detachment. Based on this, Trosman logically concludes that these fantasies were connected to Freud's later discoveries, namely the importance of oedipal sexual desires and the need to conceal such morally reprehensible ideas and feelings (Trosman, 1978, p. 218). Given that he began to take notes on his emotional life and thoughts at the age of fourteen, in his letters to Silberstein and his diary, the need to efface any traces of the documents linked to his adolescence by burning them, as a kind of *coup de grace* aimed at his future biographers, becomes clearer.

Trosman (Ibid.) suggests that the method of free-association was there already in Freud's youth, until its memory traces were elicited by his patients as an effect of transference. Because he initially relied on hypnosis, it took several years for these residues to reach the barrier of repression and, through a slow work of elaboration, coalesce in the fundamental rule of psychoanalysis. This process, which gradually improved his ability to understand his patients, was linked to his first attempts at self-analysis at the beginning of his adolescence, which we see in his letters to Silberstein. While in the *Studies on Hysteria* Freud argues that the choice of his patients was absolutely not a matter of personal preference, what he says in *The Interpretation of Dreams* sounds somewhat less defensive: he explains that he chose primarily "young subjects" as his clinical cases, thus bringing together self-analysis, memories of childhood and adolescence, and the clinical understanding of patients who were often adolescents themselves.

As for hypnosis, Freud (1925) remembers that when he was writing the *History of the Psychoanalytic Movement*, he recalled certain statements by Charcot, Breuer and Chrobak that may have led him to adopt this method of studying neurosis much earlier. However, he simply did not understand what they were trying to say and no doubt they have said more than they knew themselves or could have argued. The effects of repression are patent here: "What I heard from them lay dormant and inactive within me, until the chance of my cathartic experiments brought it out as an apparently original discovery" (Freud, 1925, p. 24). We shall later see that hypnosis was likewise linked to a spectacle Freud attended as a student.

3.7 Caesar and Brutus, a drama scene of fratricide and parricide

The dream of *Non vixit* (Freud, 1900, p. 421) revives another cultural reference of his youth: "Thus I had been playing the part of Brutus. [. . .] Strange to say, I really did once play the part of Brutus" (Freud, 1900, p. 424). In a letter to Emil Fluss, Freud speaks about the little theatre performance at his parents' house during the Purim holiday, which fell on 13th March 1870 – a date forever sacred, he jokes, because it was the day that Caesar was murdered. Schur (1972, p. 206–207) tells us that on the occasion of Freud's nephew John visiting Vienna, he and Freud played Caesar and Brutus, based on a dialogue from Schiller's play *The Robbers*

(1781) rather than on Shakespeare's *Brutus and Cassius*. The theme of Schiller's tragedy is the hatred and rivalry between two brothers: the younger is deformed and ugly, while the older is physically beautiful, a natural leader. All the tragedy that follows stems from the actions and intrigues of the younger brother, who is led astray by a Demon (the Fate), a term Freud uses in 1895 when, having carried out the first systematic analysis of a dream, he refers to Fliess as *Daimonie*. The older brother gains his father's affection and the love of a female cousin who represents a sister. Father is imprisoned in a tower by the "bad son" and, despite being rescued by the "good one", he dies of exhaustion shortly after. The grieving hero is then looking for a revenge, while his brother listens to the words of a priest, telling him that parricide and fratricide are the two truly unforgivable crimes, thus provoking his suicide. The older brother becomes the leader of a band of robbers who resemble Robin Hood's Merry Men. Interestingly, while the main character tolerates his men's looting and sets fire all around the town to save one of them from the gallows, he also presents himself as a redeemer: he wears four rings, each standing for a villain burned in the name of justice. He proclaims himself a revolutionary devoted to making Germany a republic, compared to which Rome and Sparta will be as mere nunneries. When he realises his actions have been disgraceful, he confesses that it was madness to want to right the world through crime and maintain law through anarchy. Driven by the guilt for his alleged misdeeds, he kills both his beloved and himself. The author is clearly sympathetic to his guilty hero and tries to make him a likeable character.

Schiller's play is full of familiar themes, but let's take a look at the Roman tragedy from Freud's original dream. Caesar calls Brutus his "son" and declares that he has become the greatest of the Romans by plunging his sword into his father's heart. Brutus replies that he knows only one man equal to the great Caesar – himself – and ends by saying that where Brutus lives, Caesar must die. Freud dreams that both Caesar and Brutus are *revenants*, and associates this with his satisfaction of having survived his friendship with Fliess, another great figure of the "frenemy" and a condensation of his relationship with his peers and his father. He adds:

> But the revenants were a series of reincarnations of the friend of my childhood. It was therefore also a source of satisfaction to me that I had always been able to find successive substitutes for that figure; and I felt I should be able to find a substitute for the friend whom I was now on the point of losing: no one was irreplaceable.
>
> (Freud, 1900, p. 485)

Friendship is not only marked by ambivalence and rivalry; it is also a site of loss and rediscovery. As in the dream of the cupboard, where Freud finds his mother once again beautiful and slim, the lost friends haunt him as revenants. These phantoms are an indication of a painful and unresolved mourning: ghosts are those who refuse to accept their own death, remaining forever suspended between the two worlds. Some of the satisfactions linked to his dream appear as forms of reassurance against loss: after the idea that no one is irreplaceable, another formula resonates as a kind of fantasy guarantee: "There are nothing but revenants: all those we have lost come back!" (Freud, Ibid., p. 486).

The theme shared by the two stories is the figure of parricide, which is consistent with Freud's idea of Caesar and Brutus as a model of rivalry and ambition. Speaking about an obsessional patient to whom analysis revealed his own hostile wishes hidden behind his love for his father and his worries of the latter's death, he quotes Brutus: "'As Caesar loved me, I weep for him; as he was fortunate, I rejoice at it; as he was valiant, I honour him; but, as he was ambitious, I slew him'" (1909, p. 180). He adds that these words appear strange because we would expect Brutus' affection for Caesar to be more intense. The childhood feud with John lives on, sublimated by literature. The role of Brutus condensates Freud's fratricidal and parricidal wishes, the contiguity of which I have emphasised elsewhere (Houssier, 2013).

While he identified with Brutus, the associations with John's return in adolescence can also be understood as a game of sublimation with a reversible scenario: the ambition of becoming a great man, which resonated on the oedipal level, also mobilised his fantasies of castration and murder vis-à-vis the person who might take offence at such ambition, namely his father. This ambitious fantasy, aiming to dethrone the almighty Caesar, fuelled an idealised relationship with the paternal figure. The frequent reoccurrence of this ambivalence in the father-son relationship throughout Freud's entire body of work suggests that it was constantly revived as time went by and new relationships were forged. Its conflict seems all the more permanent because, despite the idealisation – or perhaps precisely as its echo – his own father was fragile and unable to carry out one of his key roles, namely, to protect the family from the ordeals of poverty.

3.8 Student memories: from Trieste to Athens

Freud's personal education, greatly valued since childhood but cultivated essentially in his youth, became part of his memories that continued to haunt him years after. The strange experience of derealisation or the feeling of the uncanny in his personal history made him retrace his steps in order to resolve what could not have been elaborated at the time. In this sense, two classic texts of psychoanalytic literature can be put in dialogue with each other. His 1936 letter to Romain Rolland (Freud, 1936) contains a number of memories from his secondary school, which are connected to the unique moment of standing on the Acropolis alongside his brother Alexander. The essay on *The Uncanny* (Freud, 1919) demonstrates the link between the psychic upheaval of adolescence and the uncanny strangeness of one's own body.

Let's start with the latter text, where Freud talks about one hot summer afternoon he spent strolling through the empty streets of a small Italian town. In the windows of the little houses, he saw painted women, and quickly left the street. However, after having wandered aimlessly for a while, he found himself back where he had started, in the same street, which he quickly left again – only to arrive there yet a third time by another detour. He was then overcome by an uncanny feeling and, to his great relief, eventually found a familiar piazza (Ibid., p. 239–240).

This account of a commonplace phenomenon, of looking for a way out but instead constantly retracing one's steps, provoked a distressing sense of claustrophobia, of the endless return of the same. On the narrow spectrum between the uncanny and depersonalisation, Freud notes the prominence of bodily disorders in fairy tales and other fantastic literature, which is peppered with dismembered limbs, severed heads or hands cut off at the wrist. He highlights the close link between the uncanny and the detached, autonomous body part, such as the dancing feet in Schaeffer's novel *Josef Montfort*.

In relation to this, Freud alluded to his shyness when writing to his friend Silberstein that "the nonsensical Hamlet in me" prevented him from speaking to Gisela, the young girl he fell in love with (Freud, 1871–1881, p. 16). This crossing between a literary reference and his feelings is common in his writing, where the former is a favourite way of illustrating and containing the latter. How not to think of "To be or not to be" in this context, where the lovestruck Freud undergoes a kind of depersonalisation? This reference, echoing the question of identity key to the process of adolescence, is probably not accidental in young Freud's psychic life: his shyness, intense emotions and attempts at elaborating a sense of sexual identity point to the heart of Shakespeare's drama.

However, let's not lose sight of the essential. This is but a hypothesis, but could we link the memory of this strange afternoon with what he told Silberstein in their correspondence on leaving for Trieste. The repeated visits to this city marked the beginning of Freud's scientific career; his research there resulted in his first scientific publication (Freud, 1877). To his friend he confided that he saw women of loose morals, pregnant and made up like prostitutes. He was thus thrown off balance by a kind of visual vertigo, confronted with sexuality that was both exhibited and accessible. The fact of constantly returning to the place where women are freely on display betrays both a fear of women as objects of desire – fleeing them – and its contrary, a desire for sex and sexual liberation.

The link with the experience on the Acropolis naturally became part of this associative chain of memories, when it was again a question of starting a journey from Trieste, a place imbued with fantasies for young Freud, with the sexual dimension again taking centre stage. Based on his experience on the Acropolis in 1904, which until his letter to Rolland had remained enigmatic (Freud, 1936), he theorised these confusing feelings using his topographic model.

The perceptive doubt that seized him on seeing Athens and the Acropolis initially had to do with his sense of just how far he had come:

> I only doubted whether I should ever see Athens. It seemed to me beyond the realms of possibility that I should travel so far – that I should "go such a long way". This was linked up with the limitations and poverty of our conditions of life in my youth.
>
> (Freud, 1936, p. 246–247)

He adds that his dreams of travel betrayed an intense desire "to escape from that pressure, like the force which drives so many adolescent children to run away from home" (Ibid.). Once again, the memory was tainted with a sense of malaise; his wish to escape was related to the suffocating life of a traditional family, in which he was dreaming about the open seas, following the heroic fantasies of his self-narrative:

> I had long seen clearly that a great part of the pleasure of travel lies in the fulfilment of these early wishes – that it is rooted, that is, in dissatisfaction with home and family. When first one catches sight of the sea, crosses the ocean and experiences as realities cities and lands which for so long had been distant, unattainable things of desire – one feels oneself like a hero who has performed deeds of improbable greatness.
>
> (Ibid.)

This brilliant destiny was all the more important because young Freud felt as if surveilled by the narrow circle of his family and burdened with his parents' expectations, which he interiorised by becoming the family's main breadwinner.

Reading made him dream of other horizons, but he recognises the limits of his wishful fantasies; he stresses that "seeing something with one's own eyes is after all quite a different thing from hearing or reading about it" (Ibid., p. 241). As a student, he writes, he was convinced of the historical reality of Athens, were it not for an unconscious refusal which made the encounter with the Acropolis all the more disturbing when an unconscious fantasy – this city and its history do not exist – and perception collapsed into each other.

> It is one of those cases of "too good to be true" that we come across so often. It is an example of the incredulity that arises so often when we are surprised by a piece of good news, when we hear we have won a prize, for instance, or drawn a winner, or when a girl learns that the man whom she has secretly loved has asked her parents for leave to pay his addresses to her.
>
> (Ibid., p. 242)

The work of defensive reconstruction makes him forget to also include the young man's feelings of love; as the encounters with Gisela and Martha indicate, in his case this "too good to be true" manifested primarily in the field of love and sexuality.

The following sentence can therefore give rise to multiple readings:

> When I recall the passionate desire to travel and see the world by which I was dominated at school and later, and how long it was before that desire began to find its fulfilment, I am not surprised at its after-effect on the Acropolis.
>
> (Ibid., p. 243)

Contrary to his friend Silberstein's situation, the relative delay of Freud's post-adolescent sexual experience with Martha gives the fulfilment of this desire, when it at last comes true, a quasi-magical character. It is no accident that the figure of the father returns in the conclusion to his letter to Rolland, at first via a cultural reference:

> You remember the famous lament of the Spanish Moors "Ay de mi Alhama" ["Alas for my Alhama"], which tells how King Boabdil received the news of the fall of his city of Alhama. He feels that this loss means the end of his rule. But he will not "let it be true", he determines to treat the news as "non arrivé".
>
> (Ibid., p. 246)

Citing the Spanish original of the text in question, Freud concludes that the King kills the messenger – often a young man – in order to defend himself against a painful feeling of powerlessness. Like in the scene of Caesar and Brutus, the use of a cultural reference is a sublimation, a way of speaking personally or even intimately without fully revealing himself.

Adolescence and its memories return to the paternal figure, with a hint of pride, but also a death wish:

> I might that day on the Acropolis have said to my brother: "Do you still remember how, when we were young, we used day after day to walk along the same streets on our way to school, and how every Sunday we used to go to the Prater or on some excursion we knew so well? And now, here we are in Athens, and standing on the Acropolis! We really have gone a long way!" So too, if I may compare such a small event with a greater one, Napoleon, during his coronation as Emperor in Notre Dame, turned to one of his brothers – it must no doubt have been the eldest one, Joseph – and remarked: "What would Monsieur notre Père have said to this, if he could have been here to-day?"
>
> (Ibid., p. 247)

Infantile idealisation is replaced by a note of contempt that, as Freud suggests, only imperfectly hides his parricidal wish:

> As an addition to this generally valid motive there was a special factor present in our particular case. The very theme of Athens and the Acropolis in itself contained evidence of the son's superiority. Our father had been in business, he had had no secondary education, and Athens could not have meant much to him. Thus what interfered with our enjoyment of the journey to Athens was a feeling of filial piety. And now you will no longer wonder that the recollection of this incident on the Acropolis should have troubled me so often since I myself have grown old and stand in need of forbearance and can travel no more.
>
> (Ibid., p. 247–248)

Here we have young Freud's conflict condensed: the remains of filial piety and idealisation versus the murderous fulfilment of his sexual desire. The symbolic murder is carried out specifically by highlighting father's lack of education, which Freud himself made the cornerstone of his judgment of others, as we shall see in the episode of meeting Gisela and her mother. However, in order to possess a woman sexually, one must disregard the paternal authorisation, just like when one travels further than father himself could or would have imagined. In his fantasies, Freud overcomes his father by a hundred cubits, while simultaneously repairing father's lack of professional ambition. Travelling is closely intertwined with conquering new spaces, new women and ultimately becoming the hero, the seducer he never was, were it not for his dominant position at the heart of the psychoanalytic movement.

3.9 Writing like a German stylist

Between his schoolboy aphorisms and the letters written some years later after having passed his leaving exam, Freud made great progress in the development of his talents (Eissler, 1978). His friendships did not take away from his search for paternal substitutes; Hammerschlag, his religious teacher at middle and secondary school, represented both friendship and the positive aspects of his relationship with his father; together they could discuss Martha and Freud would also sometimes accept a loan. As a student, Freud was supported by Hammerschlag financially, which he found very difficult (Eissler, 2006).

Hammerschlag's daughter Anna was later the godmother of Anna Freud, who may also have been named after her. Following her marriage, Anna Lichtheim became known as Freud's patient Irma (Freud, 1900). After Hammerschlag's death, Freud praised his spirit of the great Jewish prophets and the ideal of humanism of the German classical writers (1904). The Hammerschlags lived in the same building as Breuer. Freud's daughter Sophie also shared her name with one of Hammerschlag's nieces, whom Freud was friendly with.

At the age of seventeen, young Freud had an exceptional command of language. On 16th June 1873, he writes to the brother of Gisela Fluss and his friend, Emil, that after a German composition he was happy to be told by his teacher that he had an *idiotic* style – meaning "personal", from the Greek *idios* – both correct and distinctive. Surprised by his teacher's praise, he repeated this to everyone around him and started considering himself a "German stylist", suggesting that Emil keeps their letters in case he becomes famous. "And now I advise you as a friend, not as an interested party, to preserve them – have them bound – take good care of them – one never knows" (Freud, 1871–1881, p. 4), he writes, in anticipation of his future fame and the good fortune of his biographers. The day after, his letter expresses his excitement on reading Sophocles' *King Oedipus*, which he singles out among the classic Latin and Greek texts he was obliged to study.

There is no indication of a similar talent in his family, except for Freud's father's sophisticated and elegant writing in Hebrew. Each time a relationship became personal, with Martha or with his close friends, an epistolary relationship was initiated, allowing Freud to share his thoughts and feelings freely.

The testimonies of some of Freud's acquaintances have suggested that he did indeed dream of becoming a writer, an idea he was always quick to dismiss; nevertheless, starting from the letters from his youth, his correspondence represents an informal body of work attesting to both a talent and a desire to write. As to his secret desire to become a writer, it returned repeatedly and in significant ways, whether it was later in private conversations with certain of his colleagues or in his own writing, for instance in the form of short poems and "novels" sent to his friend Eduard.

3.10 Heinrich Braun, another inseparable friend

Freud met Braun (1854–1927) in the first year of secondary school, the day of the first school report and they became inseparable. Braun's influence on him is apparent in terms of Freud's interest in studying law; when choosing his future career, his attention to social and even political matters was still very keen: "Under his influence I also decided at that time to study law at the university", he writes (Freud, 1873–1939, p. 380). Fifty years after their meeting, he said about their friendship:

> I know that I made Heinrich Braun's acquaintance during the first school year on the day of the first annual school report, and that we soon became inseparable friends. I spent every hour not taken up by school with him. [. . .] I think he encouraged me in my aversion to school and what was taught there, aroused a number of revolutionary feelings within me.
>
> (Ibid.)

Freud adds that he secretly compared Braun to a young lion.

Braun himself did not quite live up to his ambitions; he was expelled from the Leopoldstadt Gymnasium after the first four years. Instead of studying he spent most of his time in cafés, browsing foreign newspapers, which the school authorities did not appreciate. Freud himself eventually saw that the revolutionary ideals proclaimed by his friend had mostly negative aims, which created a distance between them. Braun specifically encouraged him to read books on Irish history and the history of the English culture. Freud also became friends with Braun's cousin and his own later physician Dr Ludwig Braun, a professor at the Vienna School of Medicine.

When not at school, Freud spent most of his time at Braun's, with Braun's brother and their tutor. They encouraged each other in overestimating their critical powers and superior judgment. Thanks to what he called a vague perception of youth, Freud understood that his friend possessed something more precious than academic success, namely a personality, "but it was understood that I would work with him and never let down his side" (Ibid., p. 379). Braun, who came from a wealthy background, gave Freud access to his large library; this had a decisive influence on the latter's ways of seeing the world (Eissler, 1978). However,

Freud's taste for social activities ceded under the influence of Darwin and the popular lecture given by Brühl, shortly before Freud's final exam, on the essay on *Nature* attributed to Goethe.

In Freud's memory, the word "inseparable" that he uses to characterise his and Braun's relationship (and which often appears in his prose) should be understood primarily on the emotional level. He forgets that there was in fact already a two-year separation when Braun was sent by his father to study in Leipzig, from 1867 to 1869. In 1873, after the *Matura*, Braun started university.

In 1927, Heinrich Braun's widow asked Freud about his memories for her recently deceased husband's biography. Freud answered that after having been very close in secondary school, their relationship ended at university, even though they would sometimes run into each other (1873–1939, p. 411–413). Freud was then a medical student, while Braun was studying law. In 1873, the two estranged friends met again, and Braun invited Freud to dinner with his brother-in-law Victor Adler, who was then living at 19 Berggasse, Freud's later home until his emigration. The fact that the flat had previously been rented by Adler was apparently not unrelated to Freud's later choice (Eissler, 2006). Probably under the influence of his brother-in-law, Braun, a great admirer of Bismarck, eventually decided to go into politics and later founded the newspaper *Die Neue Zeit*, the central organ of the German Social Democrats, and later a series of other journals of the same denomination.

One of Freud's patients, a boy named Albert Hirst, was intrigued by Freud's system of different entrance and exit doors, which prevented his patients from ever meeting (Houssier, 2021). Freud told him that his flat had previously belonged to the father of Victor Adler, the well-known leader of the Austrian Social Democrats. He expressed his admiration for the politician, adding that he had once visited Adler in this house. With this patient, who would have then been described as a "young man", Freud would sometimes communicate his own associations, recalling his memories of his teenage years linked to Adler and echoing the idea of living in the house of a great man.

Freud and Braun's last meeting took place in 1882, when the two men accidentally met in the street; in his letter to Frau Braun, Freud explained that even after their long separation, their discussion immediately became quite personal: Braun showed him a photo of a young girl, his fiancée, and Freud "confessed" to his own engagement.

3.11 A question of rivalry

When Freud met Wilhelm Knöpfmacher in September 1870, he positioned him among his friends as his younger brother, with Braun being his older brother. Knöpfmacher spontaneously chose Freud as his best friend. In his memory, Freud describes himself as the person who robbed Knöpfmacher of his childish beliefs. The two friends were studying together for their final exams, often spending entire nights revising at Freud's, with frugal yet appreciated provisions of coffee and grapes. After their final exam, they remained in touch: Knöpfmacher became a live-in tutor during his studies and qualified as a barrister in 1886. In a letter from 6th August 1878, Freud thanks him for a loan and sends him two articles from his "biological" period, as well as telling him, as he would to Silberstein, about his vocation of flaying animals or torturing human beings – a reference to *Max and Moritz*, an illustrated story by Wilhelm Buch (Houssier 2013).

Knöpfmacher became a member of the Jewish Vienna lodge B'naï B'rith on its founding in 1895, while Freud joined two years later. In December 1897, Freud gave a talk there, speaking about his theory of dreams for the first time before a lay public. His lecture caused quite a stir in the audience (Knöpfmacher, 1979), but also led to Knöpfmacher's dream, which Freud relates in his book on dreams (1900) as follows: Dr K comes to speak to him after his presentation, in which he understood that dreams were wish-fulfilments. On returning home, Dr K dreams that he has lost all his cases; he comes to complain to Freud. Freud evades the issue, saying that, surely, one cannot win every case, but to himself he thinks:

> Considering that for eight whole years I sat on the front bench as top of the class while he drifted about somewhere in the middle, he can hardly fail to nourish a wish, left over from his school-days, that some day or other I may come a complete cropper.
>
> (Freud, 1900, p. 152)

In his memoir, Knöpfmacher's son Hugo writes that his father never felt any rivalry towards Freud, whom he admired rather than envied; of course, one hardly excludes the other.

Years later, initiated by Julius Wagner, another classmate who became a barrister, the three men met to celebrate the sixtieth anniversary of their *Matura*. This attempt at keeping in touch with former school friends might seem surprising for Freud, but it took place at his own summer house in July 1933. They mostly reminisced about their school years, but Freud also brought up the worrisome news of late, telling them about the burning of his books in Germany and the anti-Semitic abuse of his grandson in Berlin. When he tried to have his friends guess the age of some of the antique statuettes on his desk, Knöpfmacher told him: "You keep them on your desk to feel younger," to which Freud apparently answered, as if to resist this interpretation: "He is the old one, you the young one, and I am between you two" (Knöpfmacher, 1979, p. 299).

Despite its relative prudery, Freud's adolescence was not only focused on the hero's academic development and on his friendships; the importance of these spheres and of his family life cannot occlude his preoccupation with girls, which is especially present in his correspondence at the time. As if to corroborate his later idea that adolescents tend to indulge in fantasy while awaiting the fulfilment of their sexual desires (Freud, 1905a), he experienced this period of anticipation by relying on sublimation, a path not without its upheavals and misfortunes.

Note

1 This essay, misattributed to Goethe, had a profound influence on Freud's destiny. Pestalozzi discovered that the actual author of this 1780 text was the Swiss writer G. C. Tobler. Half a century later, Goethe came across it by accident and by mistake, as a form of paramnesia, included it amongst his own works.

Bibliography

Aichhorn T. (2014), "Freud avant Freud". A propos du lycéen Sigismund/Sigmund Freud, *Adolescence*, 32(3), p. 621–640.

Börne L. (1823, 2013), *Die Kunst in drei Tagen ein original Schriftsteller zu werden*, Berlin, Hubert W. Holzinger-Verlag.

Eissler K. R. (1974), Über Freuds Freundschaft mit Wilhelm Fließ nebst einem Anhang über Freuds Adoleszenz und einer historischen Bemerkung über Freuds Jugendstil, in Eissler K. R. (dir.), *Aus Freuds Sprachwelt und andere Beiträge*, 2, Bern Stuttgart Wien, Verlag Hans Huber, Jahrbuch der Psychoanalyse, p. 39–100.

Eissler K. R. (1978), Creativity and adolescence: the effect of trauma in Freud's adolescence, *The Psychoanalytic Study of the Child*, 33, p. 461–518.

Eissler K. R. (2006), Esquisse biographique, in Eissler K., Freud E., Freud L., Grubitch Simitis I., Fleckhaus W. (dir.), *Sigmund Freud. Lieux, visages, objets*, Paris, Gallimard, p. 10–38.

Freud S. (1873–1939, 1979), *Correspondance*, Paris, Gallimard.

Freud S. (1877, 1994), Observation de la conformation de l'organe lobé de l'anguille décrit comme glande germinale mâle, in Fédida P., Widlöcher D. (dir.), *Les évolutions phylogénétiques de l'individuation*, Paris, PUF, p. 9–20.

Freud S. (1895, 1956), *La naissance de la psychanalyse*, Paris, PUF.

Freud S. (ed.). (1900), *The Interpretation of Dreams*. SE 4, London, Hogarth Press, p. ix–627.

Freud S. (1901, 1988), *Sur le rêve*, Paris, Gallimard.

Freud S. (1904), *Obituary of Professor S. Hammerschlag from Contributions to the Neue Freie Presse*. SE 9, London, Hogarth Press, p. 255–256.

Freud S. (1905a), *Three Essays on the Theory of Sexuality*. SE 7, London, Hogarth Press, p. 123–246.

Freud S. (1905b), *Fragment of an Analysis of a Case of Hysteria (1905 [1901])*. SE 7, London, Hogarth Press, p. 1–122.

Freud S. (1908), in Nunberg H., Federn E. (eds.) (1967), *Minutes of the Vienna Psychoanalytic Society, Volume 2, 1908-1910*, New York, International Universities Press, Inc.

Freud S. (1909), *Notes Upon a Case of Obsessional Neurosis*. SE 10, London, Hogarth Press, p. 151–318.

Freud S. (1910), *Contributions to a Discussion On Suicide*. SE 11, London, Hogarth Press, p. 231–232.

Freud S. (1910–1918), *Contributions to the Psychology of Love*. SE 11, London, Hogarth Press, p. 163–208.

Freud S. (1914a), *On Narcissism: An Introduction*. SE 14, London, Hogarth Press, p. 67–102.

Freud S. (1914b), *Some Reflections on Schoolboy Psychology*. SE 13, London, Hogarth Press, p. 239–244.

Freud S. (1914c), *On the History of the Psycho-Analytic Movement*. SE 14, London, Hogarth Press, p. 1–66.

Freud S. (1914–1919, 1996), *Sandor Ferenczi, Correspondance*, Paris, Calmann Levy.

Freud S. (1917, 1933), Un souvenir d'enfance dans "Fiction et vérité" de Goethe, in *Essais de psychanalyse appliquée*, Paris, Gallimard, p. 149–162.

Freud S. (1919), *The 'Uncanny'*. SE 17, London, Hogarth Press, p. 217–256.

Freud S. (1920), *A Note on the Prehistory of the Technique of Analysis*. SE 18, London, Hogarth Press, p. 261–265.

Freud S. (1925), *An Autobiographical Study*. SE 20, London, Hogarth Press, p. 1–70.

Freud S. (1926), *Karl Abraham*. SE 20, London, Hogarth Press, p. 277–278.

Freud S. (1936), *A Disturbance of Memory on the Acropolis*. SE 22, London, Hogarth Press, p. 237–248.

Freud S. (1937), *Analysis Terminable and Interminable*. SE 23, London, Hogarth Press, p. 209–254.

Freud S. (1986), *The Complete Letters to Wilhelm Fliess (1887–1904)*, Cambridge, MA, Harvard University Press.

Freud S. (1990), *Lettres de jeunesse (1871–1881)*, Paris, Gallimard.

Gedo J., Wolf E. (1976), Freud's novelas ejemplares, *Psychological Issues*, 34–35, p. 87–111.

Gicklhorn R. (1965), Eine Episode aus S. Freuds Mittelschulzeit, *Unsere Heimat*, 36, p. 18–24.

Gutton P. (1996), *Le pubertaire*, Paris, PUF.

Houssier F. (2010), *L'école d'Anna Freud. Créativité et controverses*, Paris, Editions Campagne Première.

Houssier F. (2013), *Meurtres dans la famille*, Paris, Dunod.

Houssier F. (2021), Albert Hirst, un adolescent analysé par S. Freud: sexualité, symbolisation et sublimation, *Topique*, 151, p. 33–47.

Huber G. (2009), *Si c'était Freud*, Lormond, Le bord de l'eau.

Jones E. (1958, 2006), *La vie et l'œuvre de S. Freud, T. 1: La jeunesse de Freud (1856–1900)*, Paris, PUF.

Knöpfmacher H. (1979), Sigmund Freud in high school, *American Imago*, 36, p. 283–300.

Krüll M. (1979), *Sigmund, fils de Jacob*, Paris, Gallimard.

Rodrigué E. (2000), *Freud. Le siècle de la psychanalyse*, Paris, Payot, T. 1.

Roudinesco E. (2016), *Freud: In His Time and Ours*, Cambridge, MA, Harvard University Press.

Schiller F. (1781, 1968), *Les Brigands/Die Räuber*, trad. et préf. R. Dhaleine, Paris, Aubier-Flammarion.

Schur M. (1972), *Freud: Living and Dying*, Cambridge, International University Press.

Sigmund F., Sandor F. (1996), *Correspondance (1914–1919)*, Paris, Calmann Levy.

Trosman H. (1969), The cryptomnesic fragment in the discovery of free association, *The Journal of The American Psychoanalytic Association*, 17, 489–510.

Trosman H. (1978), Freud's adolescence and the prologomena to psychoanalysis, *Journal of Youth and Adolescence*, 7(3), p. 215–222.

Winnicott D. W. (1971, 2005), *Playing and Reality*, London, Taylor & Francis.

Chapter 4

Girls

A troubling otherness[1]

Even though he recognises the traumatic aspects of the encounter with Gisela Fluss, Eissler (2006) presents a surprisingly trouble-free picture of Freud's relationship to women. He does not comment on how few women Freud was actually intimate with – according to most authors, Martha was his only lover – and argues that the founder of psychoanalysis was a complete stranger to any kind of drama, conflict or acrimonious separation, which he relates to Freud's having had a sympathetic and attentive mother. However, Freud himself did not always see his mother in this light.

Freud's love for his mother took the form of an inner permission as to his own death. When she died, Freud wrote to Fliess that he too now could die, a right he had not granted himself previously. The mother he spoke about, who connects life and death, necessarily reminds us of the mother who represents death in the dream of the Three Fates. Eissler does not discuss this idealised relationship to women when commenting on the young fiancé's jealous fits aimed at Martha and followed by periods of depression. He argues that Freud never regretted his choice, which is contradicted by the latter's indirect accusation regarding his discovery of the therapeutic potential of cocaine (Freud, 1925, p. 13–14). Martha as the exclusive choice only imperfectly conceals his wish for a more sexually liberated youth, imagined as being able to choose among several women, as I discuss later.

Eissler (2006, p. 30) also pays little attention to Martha's giving up of her interest in her husband's theory, or the effects of it: Freud slides along the symbolic equivalence, from Martha to her sister Minna and then to his daughter Anna, always choosing a love-object that is both familial and narcissistic. After the sexual passion of his first years of marriage, he was only able to love women who were interested in his theory, as illustrated by his close relationship with Lou Andreas-Salomé. With regards to his daughter, note that as a child, she was nicknamed "the black devil", a blackness that echoes with the "dark continent" as designating the enigmatic nature of female sexuality.

Gisela *Ichthyosaura* and later Martha Cordelia were thus succeeded by Anna Antigone. In this series with multiple meanings, woman as the source of mythological value puts carnal desires at a distance. In Martha's case, the symbolism of

DOI: 10.4324/9781003340898-4

these literary references (Shakespeare's *King Lear*, Sophocles' *Antigone*) requires a more precise reading: *Cordelia* is derived from the Latin *cor* (heart), followed by an anagram of "ideal". A more likely etymological origin would be the female form of "Lionheart". Another possible source might be a Gaelic word of uncertain meaning, perhaps a "jewel of the sea" or "daughter of the sea".

In Shakespeare's play, Cordelia temporarily occupies the position of the ideal daughter; she is King Lear's favourite but disappoints him so profoundly that he disinherits her. To the king's great distress, she is later killed by one of her two sisters and his illegitimate son. The father's conscious love for his daughter cannot fully hide his narcissistic infatuation; he is hurt by her sincerity, while tolerating her sisters' flattery. The three daughters' competition for the best part of the inheritance also evokes the idea of a choice among several women, a variation on being able to have sex with different partners. And lastly, let's not forget the incestuous nature of a scene in which daughters are fighting for their father's favours. Cordelia is relegated to the submissive daughter of a father gone mad, whose destiny is to be sacrificed, killed by her siblings. A similar refusal to submit is also there in the story of Antigone, which again situates Freud as a father, Oedipus, whose anti-oedipal positions create a fatal disturbance in the relationships between siblings and result in the death of his beloved daughter. Did Freud unconsciously identify with this paternal figure of Lear-Oedipus, who tends to sacrifice the women he loves?

In light of these references, Freud's relationship to women appears far from the harmonious connections described by Eissler. As a father both idealised and tyrannical, he proved to be a curse for the women around him. Is this a reversal of his sense of having been attached to women who brought him misfortune? Far from Freud's lovely vision communicated to Fliess, of having a female penchant for masculine passions, this idea rather betrays the distance he feels towards women as the source of emotional torment, as evidenced by the explosive episode of Gisela Fluss. In essence, Freud's love life would be the product of a defensive homosexuality, with an investment in his creation, psychoanalysis, as its key narcissistic identity support. If we consider this in relation to the psychoanalytic group he founded, he was indeed in the position of Lear: his students-children would fight for his favours until either killing each other or being rejected from the Freudian legacy and excluded from the psychoanalytic family. The "fantasy" of phylogenesis (Freud, 1913) represents the other side of this scenario. In the primitive horde, the banished young sons eventually come back to kill the father, who rules over women – and can freely choose among them – and the entire clan as a tyrant (Houssier, 2013).

4.1 Sexual life and its vicissitudes

Let's try to look at things in more detail. Jones (1958) left us an image of a serene and studious young man, top of his class, proud, idealistic, sporty, a good swimmer, a bookworm, in other words, any parent's ideal son, stressing that Freud's greatest pleasure as a student was his solitary walks. This official version suggests that for Freud, the emotional upheaval of adolescence was channelled into rather vague philosophical mediations and later a serious commitment to scientific principles. Jones speaks about Freud's maturity and the seemingly successful sublimations of his adolescence, concluding that his development encountered fewer obstacles than that of most young people. His lively spirit, charm and thirst for knowledge made a great impression on his entourage.

Rodrigué (2000, p. 93) is surprised by this idealised portrait: "The picture seems generally implausible. We all know about the difficulties of Freud's life, which are incompatible with the hypothesis of a serene, tranquil and above all completely asexual youth", adding that "everyone (Jones, 1958; Gay, 1991) focuses on the promise of future success, concealing our hero's solitary practices".

To support his hypothesis of Freud's adolescent sexual life, Rodrigué cites a letter to Fliess in which Freud (1887–1904) writes that neurasthenia, from which he suffers, develops in adolescence and becomes manifest between the ages of twenty and thirty. Freud associates this psychic illness, which presents especially by feelings of depression, with masturbation, the frequency of which he considers parallel to that of neurasthenia in males.

Apropos this aspect of his adolescent sexuality, let's add that masturbatory fantasies were likely to present a conflict for Freud. At one point, he answered Jones: "As a young man I felt a strong attraction towards speculation and ruthlessly checked it" (Jones, 1958, p. 32). This conflicted stance vis-à-vis his tendency to speculate, in other words, to daydream, betrays a struggle against teenage sentimental and sexual fantasies. It is reminiscent of the avoidance of intense masturbatory fantasies that may sometimes come too close to incestuous ideas, as shown in particular by his analysis of his daughter Anna (Houssier, 2010). His rejection of speculation was also part of his relationship to psychoanalysis and theory; Freud frequently worried that psychoanalysis might be judged and disqualified as a fantasy rather than science.

> When we question Freud himself, we find several key points. His appetite for knowledge about human relationships and the fight against the tendency to speculate reveal a sexual curiosity and a resistance to daydreaming. Medical studies allowed him to both satisfy his curiosity about sexuality and, forcing him to learn a certain quantity of objective facts, avoid his personal imagination,

Eissler concludes (1974, p. 78).

When Marie Bonaparte, who was very close to Freud, quizzed him on whether as a young man he had had other sexual partners or visited prostitutes, as the youth of his generation in Vienna often did, he declined to answer (Bertin, 2010). His letters to Emil Fluss, one of his friends whom he could confide in about girls, concur with this much later refusal.

4.2 Emil Fluss: the first secrets

Even though Emil was several months younger than Freud, Sigmund's letters seem to be addressed to an older and more experienced boy. This type of "older brother" transference later re-emerged in Freud's relationship with Fliess, who was also a year younger than him.

4.2.1 Let the high society know

During his secondary school years, Freud made several new friends. His friendship with Gisela Fluss' brother took the form of correspondence, already abundant in his teenage years. The letter of 18th September 1872 begins with "Dear new Friend" (1990, Ibid., p. 419) and then a warning, which returns as a constant in his letters to Silberstein: "I trust that no one will be allowed to see what was not meant for him to see", lest they make Freud write "smooth-tongued platitudes". This kind of protection of his writing is linked to feelings of shame before the parental gaze, were he to be "discovered" – which we could hear in different ways. But also, the idea of this stranger's eye, reading what was not meant for him to see, evokes the later notion of the uncanny (Freud, 1919a), which is of course closely linked to the familiar, to the point of being embodied by a parent. However, Freud's apprehension is understandable: his need for discretion is also due to the close relationship between the three families – the Freuds, Flusses and Silbersteins – and especially their mothers.

As these few letters from 1873 suggest, Freud was looking to Emil for something he had already found in Silberstein: a friend with whom to exchange secrets about girls and discuss philosophy. A particular episode stands out. To express his fascination with mother-daughter duos, Freud talks about a train journey, probably on returning from Freiberg, during which his attention was drawn to a lady and her twelve-year-old daughter. The young girl had "the face of an angel and features so neutral that she might still have turned into a beautiful page" (1990, Ibid., p. 420). He confesses his wish to "look firmly" into the girl's eyes before she was carried off by her anxious mother. He saw them again a little later, looking through the window of the train and catching a "glimpse of the blonde head with the large questioning eyes. Soon it appeared again". From then on, he could no longer take his eyes off her. She disappeared from his visual field, but he kept waiting and hoping, thinking of Freiberg. He then again saw them at the Vienna train station and promised to himself to keep on the lookout for them in town. Freud expects Emil to be disappointed that he might wish to keep this story a secret – all this fuss for nothing – and promises to tell him instead about "Ich" – an abbreviation for *Ichthyosaurus*, their code name for an important girl. In this case, the girl in question is unlikely to be Gisela, Emil's little sister, whom he can only discuss with Silberstein.

Following Emil's reply, Freud returns to the episode on the train, saying that the fact that the girl too had looked through the window showed that the curiosity had been mutual. "After all, if someone fixes us intently with his eyes, we usually return the glance with equal intensity" (Ibid., p. 421), he writes to justify this fantasy infatuation. About *Ich*, he says rather dismissively that this "flirt" was more of an occasion to share something with Emil, something to joke about, than a more serious matter. "But had you heard how the poor creature was torn to shreds", he writes about what had actually happened. He seems proud of this "masquerade", which he suggests Emil makes known to the Freiberg *haute volée*.

This encouragement that his friend shares the anecdote and even adds something to it, that he presents as fact things that one could not invent, even "have dreamt of", seems out of character. This time, Freud wants the audience – the Flusses – to have a reason to speak about them. This impulse to become the talk of the town can also be seen as an exhibitionist tendency, the opposite of secretiveness. The conflict between inhibition and exhibition would later be explored in Freud's dream-based self-analysis (Freud, 1900). As for the fleeting infatuation with the younger girl, the way he describes her suggests a repression of sexual tendencies through idealisation – the girl is a "little angel" and, because of the bisexual aspects of this attraction, she could also be a "page". Here, the account of his platonic adventure leans towards the partial drives rather than a fully sexualised seduction, which is still kept at bay, fantasised rather than enacted.

4.2.2 Fair sex, sad life

When Freud enthusiastically responds to Emil's secret attraction to the fifteen-year-old Ottilie, with whom he had gone out skating, he philosophises about the "fair sex". He praises women's lack of knowledge about the natural sciences, arguing they are born for something greater than to acquire knowledge (p. 422) – a sexually allusive statement. He is "filled with envy" (Ibid.) and tries to dampen Emil's enthusiasm by suggesting that Ottilie's concern for him may have been driven purely by "the desire to be sociable". Sarcastically, he also asks Emil whether he finds it shocking that Ottilie should learn dressmaking, unless he has already discovered the more poetic aspects of the matter. In fact, Emil later married Ottilie and had six children with her.

In his letter, Freud is not just envious or philosophical about women; he also identifies with his friend by relating a similar story which happened to him during his stay in Freiberg, in the company of his friend Eduard Silberstein, while they "represented only a minute fraction of a large group whose star was 'Ichthyosaura'". Standing in front of a weaving loom, the girl whipped away Eduard's hand as he touched the machine. For Freud, her gesture attested to "the impulse of her kind-hearted nature". Here again, it is unlikely that Freud is speaking about Gisela Fluss, which confirms that the nickname, which the three boys used as a code, was given to several girls he fell in love with.

To speak about himself, Freud mentions a bit of news that is "perhaps the most important [. . .] in my miserable life". In the following letter, he describes himself as a melancholic personality able to "suck sorrow from anything that happens", such as worrying about failing his Matura exam, because he feels irresistibly drawn to the World Exposition currently happening in Vienna. However, he also feels surer of himself and freer: when he stepped on someone's foot, the person apologised, which would not have happened previously. However, there is another reason for his increased confidence: he has decided to become a Natural Scientist and wants to "gain insight into the age-old dossiers of Nature" (Ibid., 424). On the subject of Emil's romantic pursuits, he adds: "I read Horatian odes, you live them"; the formula makes more explicit his sadness, a sense of being constrained by his sensual desires and the idea that one can be "wonderfully alone in [the] swarming crowd" of the World Exposition. This sadness is combined with the image of Emil's departure from Freiberg, which Freud imagines as a painful separation: putting himself in his friend's shoes, he speaks about having to leave one's native land and beloved parents, the most beautiful surroundings, the close-by ruins of the Hochwald castle – in other words, his own experience of loss. This nostalgic evocation, which later returns in his text on the screen-memories (Freud, 1899), leads him to conclude, this time fully aware of his identification: "I must stop, or I'll be as sad as you" (Ibid.).

Having explained that "the magnificence of the world rests, after all, on this diversity of possible alternatives, except that unhappily this does not provide a firm basis for selfknowledge" (Ibid.), he suggests that if Emil cannot understand what he is trying to say, he should let his thoughts roam free, as suggested by Börne. In the following letter, Freud looks at Emil's predicament much more positively: he asks him to relate the rest of his adventures and shows interest in the results of his daring conjectures. This differentiates their relationship particularly from the exclusivity required from Silberstein. Is this why Freud lost contact with Emil Fluss? Or was it simply that after the Matura, their academic paths diverged?

4.3 The weight of sexual prohibitions

Adding to this solitary picture, Eissler (1978) points out that Freud's first experience of love, which was completely platonic and involved a young girl named Gisela Fluss, was also to remain the only one for the next ten years. According to Clark (1985), the fact that in Freud's autobiographical writings there are virtually no references to women during his adolescence means that the man who later revealed the importance of sexuality to mental illness was particularly asexual. Roudinesco (2014) takes a different perspective, arguing that Freud preferred unfulfilled desire to physical enjoyment. I believe that we should question both of these narratives, given what Freud later said to his fiancée Martha Bernays. Three years after having met her in 1882, he writes to her:

> Did I ever tell you that Gisela was my first love when I was but 16 years old? No? Well, then you can have a good laugh at me, firstly on account of my taste and also because I never spoke a meaningful, much less an amiable word to the child.

> (Ibid., p. 419)

Freud's inhibition, to put it mildly, suggests a phobic tendency that is neither desexualised nor the expression of a conscious preference; on the contrary, it betrays a conflict between desire and defence, highlighting the weight of the prohibitions against the fulfilment of his sexual wishes. On a similar note, Boehlich (1990) believes that the external social and economic issues experienced by Freud in his youth pale in significance before his self-imposed deprivations, especially in the realm of sexuality.

What we know about Freud's sexual life prior to his encounter with Martha is largely based on his correspondence with Eduard Silberstein, thus creating a close link between friendship and love. Eduard, who was more comfortable both financially and in the games of love and sexuality, was less constrained, and this difference created a certain degree of tension between them, with Freud at times judgmental of his allegedly too frivolous friend. Hamilton (2002) shows that the designation, in their correspondence, of women as "principles" accentuates the defensive nature of Freud's idealisation of girls. For Stanescu (1965), the term "principle" used by the two friends can mean a girl, a love affair or a flirt, depending on the context.

Hamilton also notices the "psychic twinship" (2002, p. 890) that characterised Freud's friendship with Silberstein, linking them to his future relationships to Fliess and Jung. The figure of the "frenemy" returned regularly throughout Freud's life; we can take Hamilton's idea a step further and also add Ferenczi's name to this series (Houssier, 2016).

4.4 An immortal principle

Gallo (2009) points out that when Freud discusses Gisela in his letters, he uses German to speak about rational, philosophical and abstract ideas and Spanish to speak about feelings, love and attraction. Only just mentioning Gisela makes Freud switch from German to Spanish in the midst of a sentence.

Krüll (1979) associates *Ichthyosaura* with Gisela Fluss's surname, meaning "a river"; however, Freud was probably familiar with the drinking song composed in 1854 by Victor von Scheffel, about an Ichthyosaurus swimming in the sea along the forests of calamites and complaining bitterly of modern corruption. For Boehlich (1990), *Ichthyosaurus* and *Iguanodon* originate in the poem of this author, popular in the student circles of Freud's time.

Gallo (2009) returns to the crux of the matter: whether the nickname stands for Gisela or girls in general, the interpretation of this adolescent neo-language leans towards the same meaning: the fear of women and their dangerous power over men. From another angle, Boehlich (1990) understands the Freud's constant demands for exclusivity, his great need for intimacy with another person, as a way of avoiding the risk of maternal intrusion. This argument points towards the image of an anxious mother, associated through the Ichthyosaurus with a female poison, a fear of poisoning. Freud signed off one of his letters to Eduard as "Lord of the Lias and Prince of the Cretaceous", citing the end of the Saurians, animals who rebelled against the natural order but could not prevent the final catastrophe of their extinction.

It is true that Freud seems much more lyrical and romantic with Eduard than with Gisela, speaking to him with a passion that borders on the language of love. "We learned Spanish together, had our own mythology and secret names, which we took from some dialogue of the great Cervantes", he later wrote to Martha (Freud, 1873–1939, p. 96). The two secret names were Cipion and Berganza, from Cervantes' *The Dialogue of the Dogs*. While Freud wrote in Spanish to speak about Gisela and in German for Eduard, Spanish was also the language of literature, the language of Cervantes, the author of the romance between Don Quixote and Dulcinea. Gallo argues that Spanish was the language of fantasy, of imagination, while Freud's affection for Eduard was real, alive, with feelings too intense to be spoken about in any but his native tongue.

In his paper on the *Screen-Memories*, Freud (1899) confirms that he returned to Freiberg at sixteen or seventeen. However, in a letter to Emil Fluss from 7th February 1873, he talks about something that happened on this visit to Freiberg two years previously; this led Grubrich-Simitis (1984) to argue that Freud was off by a year and the visit happened in 1872. However, as the author himself points out, it is unlikely for us to forget if an event took place one or two years previously – unless we wish to conceal something quite intimate. Because Freud's mother went for treatment for her tuberculosis to Roznau and Freud spent his holidays during secondary school there, he may have visited Freiberg, only 25 km away, on other occasions. The two families, the Silbersteins and the Freuds, were very close: Anna Silberstein and Amalia Freud regularly met at the spa in Roznau to take waters and discuss their domestic problems.

Thus there are several versions as to when Freud first met Gisela; without going into the details of this debate, I will stick to the version I consider most plausible, which is the one presented by Boehlich (1990). During the summer of 1871 the Freuds were staying with the Flusses. Having met the young girl, who was then twelve, for the first time during this summer, Freud again saw her in the following year, 1872, this time without his friend Eduard but together with another mutual friend, Ignaz Rosanes. Freud made friends with Gisela's brother Emil and fell desperately in love, while feigning indifference by trying to trivialise things through humour and irony. "This juvenile irruption of sexuality seems to have made him uneasy, like other attacks later on", Boehlich comments (Ibid., p. 23). Roudinesco (2014) sees this as the contradictions fuelling Freud's ambivalence towards sexuality: on the one hand, a tendency to eroticise all intrafamily relations and even make up transgressions and turpitudes that only existed in his imagination; on the other hand, a repression of his drives. In my understanding, it is because the permeability of repression in adolescence renders such incestual fantasies all the more disturbing, the violence of the most burning desires must be suppressed. Freud's friendship with Eduard, which is tinged with sublimated homosexuality, shows us a displacement of such suppressed tendencies onto this relationship through intellectual interests and sublimation. Intellectualisation or asceticism, but also trivialisation, irony and even contempt, are ways of containing these drives, while the parricidal and incestuous fantasies are being elaborated, before the encounter with a woman – Martha – becomes possible. While Freud fell in love with both mother and daughter, it was his father who introduced him to the Flusses (whose name phonetically resembles that of Fliess), according to the information obtained by Bernfeld (1951) from one of the family's sons. We hardly need to add that Freud fell in love with Gisela in his native town, forging a direct link with his love for his mother?

4.5 Gisela, a potentially traumatic love at first sight

As an adult, to describe the only love story of his boyhood, Freud (1899) pretends to be a thirty-eight-year-old patient remembering his first love, a sudden passion for a girl of fifteen. After their short meeting, the young girl returned to school and this separation only exacerbated his longing.

> I passed many hours in solitary walks through the lovely woods that I had found once more and spent my time building castles in the air. These, strangely enough, were not concerned with the future but sought to improve the past.

The past is enhanced through this idealisation. His "double" describes his regrets as: "If only I had stopped at home. (. . .) And then if only I had followed my father's profession and if I had finally married her – for I should have known her intimately all those years!" (Ibid., p. 313), as if to show that the father's symbolic endorsement may have been missing at the time. Left without this possibility of identification, Freud convinces himself, with much regret, that he could have loved Gisela in reality as much as he loved her in his fantasies.

To Eduard, he writes that he did not suffer any conflict between the ideal and reality, and is unable to make fun of Gisela (Freud, 1871–1881). Behind the veneer of courtly love, the surge of adolescent desires makes him afraid of immoral and reprehensible acts, which inhibits even the most innocuous ways of relating to her. While the dialogue with his "patient" revolves around the "bold fantasies" of deflowering, the desires and "coarsely sensual" fantasies of a "young scapegrace" (Freud, 1899, p. 315–316), these contrast completely with his shyness during their actual encounter. We can follow the associative link between the child who will "come to nothing", in the words of his father, and the "good-for-nothing" adolescent doubting his own intelligence, his narcissistic value, so much so that he sabotages himself.

The fantasy of deflowering a young virgin and its sadistic nature have been identified by Anzieu (1959) and Rocah (2002); Freud's case-like reconstruction highlights the fact that he considered this love story primarily as a symptom. However, things seem even more complex.

One of the main goals of the Academia Castellana, the philosophical society created with Silberstein, was to have a secret language to speak about girls. After Freud's return to Freiberg and the Flusses without his friend, he writes to his friend about the phobic avoidance linked to his infatuation: "Instead of approaching her I have held back" (Freud, 1871–1881, p. 12), stressing that she knows nothing about his feelings for her. He is not afraid of Eduard finding his behaviour ridiculous, since he "knows that people are altogether brutish and foolish" (Ibid.). The excessive intensity of his passion provokes harsh self-criticism, which spares him the shame of ridiculousness but not self-incrimination, including the fear of madness, one of the typical anxieties of adolescence. In the following letter, Freud protests against his friend having called his mood "gloomy and sad", blaming it instead on his "nonsensical style, which [. . .] never allows me to say what I mean" and rejecting the nevertheless probable hypothesis of his depressiveness. The letter is tinged with ambivalence previously occluded by his idealisation of his beloved. The experience with Gisela arguably forced young Freud to take drastic defence measures against the impulses of his heart. Already the nickname *Ichthyosaura* suggests an unconscious fear of women: this prehistoric animal is a dangerous monster threatening to engulf everyone else (Eissler, 1978). The narcissistic dimension of his idealised love is revealed already in the "Ich" of Gisela's nickname. As also evidenced by his relationship with her mother, for young Freud the beloved had to be someone who resembled him, a type of object-choice he would later designate as narcissistic (Freud, 1914).

In this context, the relationship with Martha appears as a kind of compromise to his childhood and adolescent conflicts (Rodrigué, op. cit.): finding a refuge for the drive rather than taking the risk of a devouring passion, which was nonetheless there at the beginning of their relationship, during their separation. And there is another element: his wish to become a man of importance, to make good on his oedipal promise, runs into an obstacle. Only romantic passion can divert him from his path, which is more narcissistic than anaclitic and satisfies (or repairs?) his parents. He writes to Eduard (Freud, 1871–1881, p. 19): "Gisela's image refused to budge from my mind. Caramba!" The Spanish exclamation usually expresses anger and at long last lets out some of the hyper-condensed instinctual steam.

The account of the incident tries to make light of Freud's feelings – and yet, when the "Rat Man" pronounced Gisela's name some thirty-five years later, Freud added three exclamation marks to his written account (Freud, 1909). The Rat Man told him that during the manoeuvres, he heard Captain Nemecek mention a certain Gisela Fluss. In a footnote, the editor wonders whether one of Gisela's brothers had not married a girl also called Gisela. As for Freud, he concluded that the Rat Man liked to masturbate while fantasising about her.

It is likely that the Gisela experience indeed had a traumatic effect (Eissler, 1978), as it may sometimes happen with sudden infatuations. This intense and overwhelming albeit short-lived love story appeared like a thunderbolt in not quite a serene sky.

4.6 Looking for daughter, finding mother

Freud's investment in Gisela did not end with the painful feelings of disappointment and inhibition; it also involved an extension of the libido from daughter to mother – unless unconsciously it was the other way around. Telling Eduard about his crush, he praises Gisela's mother, repeating how nice and hospitable, how good and noble she is to have introduced him "into her family circle". He complains to his friend about his toothache, which he tried to treat with some pure alcohol on an empty stomach, assisted by Emil in his dye shop. He then "passed out" (p. 18), so that Emil had to carry him upstairs, where he vomited the undigested alcohol and Gisela's mother cared for him "as for her own child". The doctor was called and the next morning Frau Fluss laughed when he said he had not slept a wink but did not notice she came to see him twice during the night. "I felt ashamed", he comments; he did not deserve all this kindness and goodness. This is a first displacement, a desexualisation of the "mad" genital impulse. In this maternal attention, caring for his toothaches and vomiting, Freud finds the image of a tender mother which masks the adolescent's sexual desires.

To Silverstein he writes about Gisela: "I [. . .] flinch slightly when her mother mentions Gisela's name at table [. . .] only the nonsensical Hamlet in me, my diffidence, stood in the way of my finding it a refreshing pleasure to converse with the half-naive, half-cultured young lady" (Ibid., p. 16). This indicates, fleetingly but precisely, the fall of idealisation, where the love-object has been infiltrated with ambivalence, prompting comparisons between the daughter and her mother, Eleonora Fluss, then aged thirty-eight.

This ideal mother, who facilitated the transformation of passionate love for the daughter into a "cooler" friendship with her respectable mother, came from a middle-class background; she had once lived in difficult conditions, but acquired an education "of which a nineteen-year-old salon-bred young thing need not be ashamed". The reference to a well-bred young woman necessarily conjures the young Freud's female double, both in terms of their life trajectories and the value put on personal education. "Need not be ashamed" adds a more personal tone, for someone so preoccupied by his own image, at risk of being "damaged" were his secrets to be revealed. Like him, Gisela's mother is well-read, including the classics, a comment betraying a narcissistic satisfaction, concluding that "hardly a branch of knowledge [. . .] is foreign to her". It is her who brings a sense of modernity into the house; she participates in the social and political affairs in Freiberg – a far cry from the ill and plaintive mother Freud later describes in his correspondence with Martha. He alludes to this comparison when he says that Frau Fluss is not a "frustrated bluestocking". Praising her authority, he says apropos her seven children that "no concern of any of them ceases to be hers" (Ibid.). He has never seen "*such* superiority". Returning to Eduard, he laments that while their respective mothers take care of their physical well-being, they have done nothing for their intellectual life. Gisela is in a position comparable to Freud's; like him, she was her mother's favourite, which he connects to the fact of her broader education. In terms of child-rearing, she prefers to act on feelings rather than physically disciplining her children.

The comparison with his own mother returns in another form: Frau Fluss "fully appreciates that I need encouragement before I speak or bestir myself, and she never fails to give it", so that he ends up following her lead. What Freud sees as "superiority" appears as a need for authority and support, the lack of which he seems to feel from his parents. Although Frau Fluss is not particularly pretty, she has a "witty, jaunty fire" that emanates from her. Gisela takes after her father as well, but her "wild beauty" is her mother's.

4.7 Living through the Oedipus complex before its discovery

Freud thus discovered, long before theorising it, the existence of erotic trans-ference and of what he would later call the Oedipus complex: "[I]t would seem that I have transferred my esteem for the mother to friendship for the daughter. [. . .] I am full of admiration for this woman whom none of her chil-dren can fully match." The discovery of this transference to the mother was later theorised when he argues that transference establishes itself spontane-ously in all human relationships. Schacht (2006), who sees Freud's feelings for mother and daughter as interchangeable, suggests that Freud desired both rather than one or the other as a substitute.

The author bases her claim on the toothache story. Gisela's mother came into Freud's room twice and he did not even notice, thus repressing the erotic aspects of the scene. His later embarrassment on feeling that his fantasies may have been exposed when Frau Fluss laughs when he tells her he had not slept a wink, attests to the shameful, that is, incestual, nature of the fantasy summoned. Metaphori-cally speaking, he had truly only slept a wink.

The displacement from the daughter to the mother who takes care of him takes the form of a friendship which avoids the intensity of his feelings but remains marked by an idealisation comparable to his passion for Gisela. Freud both aspires to and recognises himself in this female ideal. As a result, this shift helps devalue the love-object itself, because Gisela cannot measure up to her mother's admired perfection. Like Freud, Eleonora is cultured, she is well read and a good conversa-tionalist. Freud cannot reproach himself for feeling a friendship for a mother who knows how to "give orders" and "plays as large a part in running the business as Herr Fluss". These are all extra protections against sensual desires: she represents authority, as if condensing the paternal and maternal figures in a single character. The parental couple is invested in the light of a primitive scene founded on their understanding, where the mother is the more dominant of the two and can even compensate for the potential professional insufficiency of her husband.

Boehlich does not seem convinced by this affection for the mother, which he considers a mere illusion. However, he does note that Eleonora had some of the qualities Amalia lacked and thus represented the mother Freud would have liked to have. Eleonora was modern, liberal, well-educated and free of the spirit of the ghetto (Boehlich, 1990, p. 23). And unlike Jacob, her husband Ignaz Fluss was able to beat the textile industry crisis. Freud thus dreamt up a double family romance: as a textile merchant, he would like to have both a father like Ignaz and a mother like Eleonora. This seems a way of distancing himself from his own father, who himself did not have to curb his sexual desires. However, one element suggests that Freud's attachment to Frau Fluss was not simply defensive, contrary to Boehlich's argument. When he writes to Emil Fluss in 1873, he makes a unique request: since Eduard's grandmother had said that she knew the Flusses, he would like to know Frau Fluss' maiden name in order to "trace the closely knit web of connecting threads which chance and fate have woven around us all" (Freud, 1871-1881, p. 421). This apparently reasonable request follows the displacement of love from daughter to mother, giving more proof, should we need it, that Freud's interest in mothers stemmed from the flames of incestuous desires – and the shame they provoked in his adolescent mind.

In my view, this sequence of displacements "saved" Freud; alongside the transference from Gisela to her mother and the parental couple, we should also include the displacement to his relationships with peers. The haunting presence of Gisela's image led to attempts at distancing, particularly through forging close friendships with Braun and Silberstein, of whom he said, using the same term, that as boys they were "inseparable". "We used to be together literally every hour of the day that was not spent on the school bench", he wrote to Martha apropos Eduard (1873–1939, p. 96).

4.8 Remembering the experience: Gisela, a third?

In one of his letters to Emil, Freud writes that he has great admiration for the "saurian myth" (1871–1881, p. 11). The attraction to myths and an identification with those who can create them are paramount here and will later find many applications: in psychoanalysis as a history, in the infantile as a search for personal prehistory, in the archaic as a constant source of theoretical and clinical interest, and finally in the creation of the psychoanalytic myth of the primal horde (Houssier, 2013). The sexual excitation provoked by the twelve-year-old girl with the face of an angel and gender-neutral features finds an echo in Gisela; in his letters, Freud refers to both of them as "a child".

For Eissler (1978), this encounter was a crucial moment in Freud's life. He suggests that the paper on screen-memories concerns, above all, his personal life, namely two separate occasions he links together. Gisela would be the screen-character of Freud's nanny, who had earned his love and then abruptly disappeared from his life when she was arrested for a series of petty thefts in the family home. This feeds into the idea of a traumatic love in Freud's life, linked to the severing of a cherished relationship. Faced with this new *coup de foudre* and the passion it engendered, Freud felt completely overwhelmed, contrary to the portrait he paints to Silberstein.

In his letters to the latter, once he moves on to the subject of "girls", this time without any metaphoric allusions, he switches back to German. This passage marks the first distancing: the topic is not worthy of their Spanish newspeak. In passing, he confirms the existence of his "diary" by confessing his attraction to Gisela. Despite her imminent departure the next day, her absence will restore "a sense of security about my behaviour that I have not had up to now" (Freud, 1871–1881, p. 12). Being in love gives him confidence, all the more so because Gisela's departure allows him to fantasise about her, to keep his love-object in mind without having to worry about the effects of their encounter. The idea of feeling more self-assured despite his shyness and the possible suffering inflicted by the object's absence now appears less contradictory. Removing this apparent contradiction strengthens the role the love affair played in his relationship with Eduard. Gisela acted as a third in the sense that Freud's attachment to her, despite its phantasmatic and projective nature, kept the spectre of homosexuality at bay. In this case, the fear of homosexual fantasies must be situated in a context of inhibited heterosexuality, which gave their friendship its intensity. This investment gave Freud something to talk about with Eduard, putting them on equal footing; they could now share the same object of concern without Freud feeling hurt by his friend's boldness and superiority in the realm of love. The fear of ridicule indicated the potential shame of feeling that, despite his academic excellence, he felt behind in this respect. The close ties between the Flusses and the Freuds, the small and quasi-familial environment, all account for the atmosphere of an extended family, which fuelled the need to conceal incestuous fantasies.

Hence the constant appeals for his friend's discretion, so that his mother does not find out anything about these matters. To his friend, he presents the "transference" of his love for Gisela to her mother as a form of respect:

> I am, or consider myself to be, a keen observer; my life in a large family circle, in which so many characters develop, has sharpened my eye, and I am full of admiration for this woman whom none of her children can fully match.
>
> (Ibid., p. 17)

The investment of the gaze has a double meaning: it has to do both with shame vis-à-vis his internalised parents and his own perspective on his family ties.

4.9 Girls: between poison and boredom

At a later time, having passed his Matura, the images of Gisela and other girls were still at the forefront of his mind. In a letter from 20th August 1873, he initiates a dialogue with Eduard about "young ladies" and the "antidote" to boredom his friend argues they represent (Ibid., p. 40). Eduard is very much in favour of dating and regularly flirts with girls. Quickly, Freud responds; but if one is healthy to start with and not easily bored by oneself, aren't young ladies just "crystallized poison of boredom" rather than an antidote? And, he wonders, are they only boring when one speaks to them in German, or also when one addresses them in French? A gap emerges between the two friends, with Eduard seemingly preoccupied with "gallantry", while Freud prefers to cultivate his mind. Girls are associated to venom, alluding to the archaic nature of the danger represented by prehistoric fish. Faced with this rejection tinged with anxiety and probably related to literature where poison is the female weapon of choice, Freud asks Eduard again and more insistently for a picture of him (which they have previously discussed), telling him that he has given up "the attachment that bound me to Gisela" (Ibid., 41). "Not because another has taken her place; indeed, that place can remain empty", he writes, unless it be "filled with something other than air". When the Flusses come to Vienna in order to help their children's education, Freud decides to "absent myself from them many times", so that "they will not miss me even more often". His desire for self-effacement, and its reverse side of megalomania, resonates with the following sentence, which sums up his position: "I have grown tired of and been led astray by this overlong game" (Ibid., 42). This idea of being led astray returns regularly. Girls are a source of angst and distraction, which Freud experiences as a guilt-inducing hindrance to his ambitions of greatness.

4.10 A ghost comes and goes

In closing the letter from October 1874, Freud refers to a visit to the Flusses a day after Eduard's departure, saying that it did not provoke much trouble for him, as he would have expected from seeing his former beloved.

In a short letter from early 1875, he again speaks about a visit from Gisela and her sister, his uncle and a friend. He says that "it all passed off fairly well" (p. 81) with regards to Gisela, who thus spent the New Year's Eve with the Freuds. He adds that only Eduard were needed to make the evening bearable.

Later, on 17th January 1875, Freud decries his friend's "unnaturally chivalrous" thoughts and emotions (Ibid., p. 82) in order to better describe his own. The following passage reminds us of his effort to curb the idealisation of girls and of Gisela in particular as a way of lessening his disappointment or even pain:

> While my chivalry is thus reduced to hollow illusions, you must still strip its image of several falsehoods intended to elevate it to a position beyond anything it might wish for itself or one you could defend before God or your conscience. Strip it of its lures, its artifices, its serpentine wiles, and its charms; it is still far from being an Armida,
>
> (p. 83)

he writes about Gisela's New Year's visit at the Freuds, an event during which he was "merrier than normal" according to "authoritative sources". The effort to free himself requires the intervention of a third party, which depersonalises his attachment to Gisela. He opposes Eduard's view of young ladies as innocent and instead believes they harbour "Mephistophelean ideas" and includes other descriptions of reptiles with venomous fangs. In a still more personal tone, he confides in his friend that "the company of ladies" continues to feel awkward to him, only to make him feel gladder that this should be the opposite for Eduard.

The reference to Armida is not accidental. Armida is a character from *Jerusalem Delivered*, by the Italian poet Torquato Tasso. She is a Muslim sorcerer,

the daughter of King Arbilan. Her most famous love affair involves the knight
Rinaldo; she falls in love with him though they are enemies. She then tries in vain
to use magic to keep his love. Her character is of interest for two reasons: first,
the figure of the "frenemy" replicates in the relationship with Gisela in the form
of the jilted lover. Second, the scene also resembles a reversal of the situation as
a means of wish fulfilment. It is Armida who falls in love and tries to entangle
Renaud in her spells, raising the question whether Freud may have experienced
being lovestruck as a form of traumatic passivation.

When he tries to convince Eduard that Gisela is no longer idealised, he main-
tains a position full of respect, the meaning of which can be understood following
the scene with Eleonora. This respect is based on romantic chivalry, which necessarily reminds us of Don Quixote and his author Cervantes, greatly admired by
both friends.

Freud is also ironic about his friend's dance lessons, which the latter seems to
enjoy more than other kinds of study; Freud tells him this will be greatly appreciated by his sisters who wish to learn "the noble art, needless to say not without the
Flusses, for what can possibly take place nowadays without the Flusses!" (Ibid.,
p. 84). He adds that Gisela and her sister Sidonia represent a model which his
sisters endeavour to emulate and these lessons will be an opportunity for Eduard
to speak to Gisela, for which he normally has little occasion.

Contrary to what various authors have argued, the relationship to Gisela was
not limited to the first moment of passion and then its memory, having met her
in town or remembering her later in life. Because of the close links between the
two families, she was a constant in young Freud's everyday life. This family
connection, cultivated above all by the two mothers, also brings up the question of Freud's relationship with his sisters, which, if we are to believe his
letters, was quite ambivalent. He could not speak more freely with Gisela also
because she became "one of the girls" in the extended family. His disappointment of being unable to break the ice was combined with his jealousy towards
his sisters, who in his eyes had access to Gisela, provoking feelings of powerlessness and envy, despite all his efforts at rejecting womenkind. His beloved
was therefore experienced as a quasi-persecutory figure, unless he was trying
to conceal his narcissistic injury in his letters. With Gisela, he was no longer
the golden child adulated by his mother; he was a lone young man responsible
for his own desires.

Gisela returns in the letter of 11th April 1875, where Freud, having written
at length about various philosophical debates, tells Eduard that if the past still
interests him, he should know that she went to Italy. But only as far as Verona, he
adds dismissively, reminding us of the importance of travel as a way of escaping
his family and surpassing his father. Since her return, she has been recounting the
details of her travels to his sisters, who relay them to Freud. Despite his attempts
at forgetting her, she thus once again comes back both physically and in speech of
his sisters, who are no doubt unaware of what she really means to him.

4.11 Man down: a principle gets married

Bernfeld (1951) argues that the defences mobilised by Freud's encounter with Gisela served to deny its implications. After a short while, passionate love gave way to despondency and grief, and finally to sarcasm and contempt. The latter is the other side of irony; both are expressions of affect guided by narcissism, attacking the other or oneself by mocking an aspect of a personality. Both conceal a dimension of importance, a cruelty towards the object.

The fleeting and projective nature of Freud's infatuation with the mother-daughter duo left him disappointed and bitter, despite the exaltation he showed to Eduard. A sentence from his later work is highly illustrative: "It is that we are never so defenceless against suffering as when we love, never so helplessly unhappy as when we have lost our loved object or its love" (Freud, 1930, p. 82). This simple statement, devoid of any meta-psychological jargon, echoes the idea of the traumatic lack of preparedness of young people previously shielded from sexuality; it is like sending them to the Arctic dressed only in summer clothes.

Gisela again reappears in a long satirical poem written to Eduard and based on the beginning of the *Odyssey* (Boehlich, 1990). The letters of 1st and 2nd October 1875, which follow the announcement of a marriage of a "principle", include an addendum, a mixture of "sadness and jest". This "nuptial" poem gives us the overall impression of sadness worked over through humour. Let's look at some of its more significant passages.

The Ichthyosaura in question "was to the Academia so bright an example" (Freud, 1871–1881, p. 136) that she was offered a prize, but the fury of the Cretaceous brought her downfall, "for nothing on earth is eternal". This girl conquers men's hearts, "leaving them lovesick"; her stature is compared to a poplar, a fir, a pine, a cedar, until she is described as the "noblest of forms, the ideal of shapes [. . .] and gloriously rounded" (Ibid.). "Sing me, oh Muse, the praises of Ichthyosaura communis", Freud writes lyrically.

But the praise is followed by a stream of invectives, revealing the young man's affliction. The idealisation of "Ich" is replaced by more negative images, for example, "that the spirit but dully moves in the sunny flesh" or "that the eye was not pierced by learning's sharp rays". Compared to insects or worms, which are later identified as the symbols of small children in dreams (Freud, 1916), these are "never plagued by the spirit" (Freud, 1871–1881, p. 138). As it is often the case, Freud's adolescent female ideal combined a physical and aesthetic attraction with a narcissistic projection of his own ideal of intelligence, his ego-ideal based on the acquisition of knowledge, making up for his feelings of being excluded from relationships with girls.

If the poet be free "to probe with a curious eye what is normally hidden from view, he will find the sphere's principle pervading the forms blessed night reveals to the fortunate groom". The principle of the forms of female beauty is here combined with Freud's ideas about the wedding night, the special moment where a romantic relationship at last becomes sexualised. The following formulation highlights his exaltation before the sexual encounter, which quickly fades into disenchantment:

> And the hastening mail that lets me not linger to describe her eyes' luster and fine inner hue [. . .] but commands one, with fleeting glance, to survey the whole maid, resplendent now, who, at one with her groom, a housewife becomes.
>
> (Ibid.)

It seems that the poem is ultimately about a young girl known to Eduard, whom Freud calls Rosenzweig ("rose" and "twig"), as if the lines addressed both Freud's young love and that of his friend. In the addendum, he expresses a wish:

> And may a new age begin without forces working in secret, that has no need of poetry and fantasy! Let no one seek a principle save in the present, not in the alluvium or diluvium, nowhere save among the children of man, not in the gruesome primeval past when wild creatures could consume the oxygen of the atmosphere unpunished by man –

Despite the enigmatic nature of some of these passages, we see a wish to distance himself from fantasy and poetry, even though he has just written a poem. This apparent contradiction restages the conflict we have previously identified with regards to Freud's tendency to speculate and fantasise, which continued torment-ing him throughout his life, including in his work.

As a psychoanalyst, Freud later understood that his excessive timidity had been linked to his aggressiveness and specifically to his fantasies around the wedding night. However, when it comes to Gisela, his chivalrous spirit seems to disappear. Eissler (1978) suggests that the reproaches made to the girl, who was innocent, were in fact addressed to himself. Freud constructed a fantasy around this particu-lar wedding announcement. As to Gisela, we know that she got married in 1881, that is, six years after this letter had been written. This does not mean that Freud could not have learnt, for example, that she had her eyes on another boy, or that the principle in the poem might not have been another girl, even though its fervour strongly recalls the intensity of young Sigismund's quiet passion.

At this particular moment, despite feeling depressed on a Sunday when he does not work, his sense of humour protects him from hurt, even though the manic triumph supposed to ensue fails on this occasion.

4.12 Return to a created biography: memory and its screens

The only text in which Freud (1899) speaks about Gisela's memory is his paper on screen-memories. Eissler (1978) highlights the particular status of this essay amongst his other works. In fact, Freud avoided any new publications until 1925, when his *Complete Works* in German were published; on this occasion, he deleted a passage from *The Interpretation of Dreams* (Freud, 1900) that may have revealed the true identity of the patient he was in dialogue with – that is, himself. The text was then not included in the first collection of his psychoanalytic works and was only cited in *The Psychopathology of Everyday Life* (Freud, 1901), despite it containing a key psychoanalytic concept, the screen-memory. Both Bernfeld and Eissler also point out that in his autobiographical works, Freud avoided any mention of his love life. It was difficult for him to go into the details of the Gisela affair. We may add to this that his infantile eroticism, as well as his rivalrous and murderous wishes appeared very clearly in the book on dreams, but what was subject to censorship was precisely the erotic life of his youth, forever marked by the Gisela episode, to which he covertly returned precisely in the text on screen-memories. In 1899, Freud had not yet said anything about his personal life, besides his date and place of birth. He took five years off his age when introducing his patient – his double – and on reading the text, we see very well his reasons to remain discreet about his intimate life as a teen. To conclude this chapter, I will take a closer look at this essay, bringing together its biographical and theoretical elements in three steps.

4.12.1 A profusion of excitations

In this paper (Freud, 1899), the story of Gisela is presented in a way that trivialises the material at hand. The case concerns a thirty-eight-year-old man, whose particular situation is the most instructive out of many similar ones. Its value is that the person is not at all or only slightly neurotic. Freud was able to relieve this "patient" of a slight phobia, probably related to his departure from his native town at the age of three. Already in the first French edition, a note indicates that the patient with whom Freud is speaking is none other than himself, leading to an imaginary narcissistic dialogue, or a kind of praise of his self-analysis.

Let's look at the familiar story by organising it more clearly around Freud's adolescence: in the childhood memory that emerges he sees a green meadow with yellow flowers, dandelions. Above the meadow, a peasant cottage and in front of its door two women are standing and chatting, a peasant-woman and a nursemaid. He is playing in the grass with his cousins: John, one and a half year older, and Pauline, who, like Freud, is three. They are picking the flowers and the two boys, who decide that the girl has the nicest bouquet, throw themselves on her to snatch it away from her. The little girl starts crying and runs to the peasant-woman, who gives her a piece of dark bread. The flowers are abandoned, and the boys also run to ask for bread, which in Freud's memory tastes delicious. "In an almost hallucinatory fashion" (Ibid., p. 312), Freud writes, the yellow colour of the flowers and the taste of the bread are remembered in an exaggerated way, as if disproportionately prominent. The supposed patient says that he recovered this memory and others thanks to another recollection, which dates back to his adolescence: at seventeen, he returned to his native town and stayed with a family with whom his own family had been friendly since his early childhood. He adds: "I must admit that there was something else that excited me powerfully" (Ibid., p. 313). He then speaks about the collapse of his father's industry and his nostalgia for the beautiful woods where he would try to run off from his father, just as he had learnt to walk – hence his frustration with city life. By the time he returned, the Flusses were doing very well professionally.

> But it is no use evading the subject any longer: I must admit that there was something else that excited me powerfully. I was seventeen, and in the family where I was staying there was a daughter of fifteen, with whom I immediately fell in love.
>
> (Ibid.)

Here again the ages have been changed, making both protagonists slightly older.

Shortly after their meeting, the young girl returned to school and this separation exacerbated his feelings of nostalgia – and loss, we could add. After his heart, his imagination was set on fire: returning to the beautiful woods of his childhood, he spent time building castles in the air, though in a retrograde fashion. These daydreams tried to improve the past rather than turning to the future, as if to fuel the adolescent family romance about his childhood. If only he had stayed in his native land, growing up to be a strong man like Gisela's brothers, he could have taken over his father's business and married the young lady. He would have loved her as much as he did in his daydreams, which in itself can be seen as an adolescent fantasy: the purity of a love "bigger than life", transposed from fantasy to reality. The latent reproach to his father implies a form of rupture in the professional lineage; Freud seems to suggest that, had his father succeeded, he would have been easier to identify with.

4.12.2 Struggling with masturbation fantasies

Twenty-seven years after meeting Gisela, Freud rediscovered feelings of similar intensity. Although his love for the daughter had been replaced by an admiration for the mother, he adds: "A strange thing. For when I see her now from time to time – she happens to have married someone here – she is quite exceptionally indifferent to me" (Ibid.). At the same time, the yellow colour of the dress she was wearing when they first met remains an indelible memory, affecting him whenever he sees the same colour anywhere else.

The childhood dress was of a yellowish-brown colour, like the wallflower. We see the primordial sensorial potency of infantile memories, linked to the nostalgia of this first love, which is maintained over time like an exceptionally intense "fueros". The indifference he now feels, which was nonetheless contradicted by his reaction to her name during the Rat Man's analysis (Freud, 1909), attest to the projective nature of this infatuation.

Later, when Freud was working hard to succeed, "struggling for [his] daily bread", "mountaineering was the one enjoyment that I allowed myself" (Freud, 1899, p. 314–315), he writes. He plays on the association between "bread" and "daily bread" to connect the memories of childhood and adolescence, where the latter appear both determined by and complementary to the former. Adolescence thus becomes a way of exploring and understanding infantile complexes.

His studies are described as an "unpractical ideal" (Ibid., p. 315). The discussion with his double gives rise to a peculiar hypothesis: the scene is not a childhood memory but rather a fantasy, retroactively inserted into childhood and based on an adolescent memory. As if the material from his early youth could be introjected into the alleged memories of childhood. The interdependence between infantile and adolescent material is thus strengthened, even though Freud passes over the question of the memory's "authenticity". The patient, his double, encourages Freud to think about the symbolic language of this childhood memory, namely the idea that taking flowers away from a girl alludes to a *deflowering*. "What a contrast between the boldness of this phantasy and my bashfulness on the first occasion and my indifference on the second", he adds as if to highlight the enigmatic nature of this infantile adolescent scene. And it is Freud's task to then corroborate this interpretation by adding that "bold" sexual fantasies are simply the complement of "youthful bashfulness" (Ibid., p. 316).

Let us pause shortly and return to the different hypotheses in this sequence. A three-year-old's phallic impulses provoked by an older boy are of course to be considered; however, could the fantasy of deflowering, probably associated with fantasies of rape, acquire such consistency without the genital fantasies of adolescence? The hypothesis of adolescence as what gives meaning, via pubertal insight, to infantile material, is a much bolder perspective. Youthful bashfulness indeed contrasts with the unbridled drives of childhood, in the sense that genital sexuality brings a radical change. The assault on a young virgin is now associated with a sexual violence which provokes a repression of the drives, a direction Freud followed in a quasi-ascetic manner. Why quasi? Because he seems to have oscillated between certain pleasures, including a fantasy life full of audacious and transgressive desires, and a more repressive position, due to the intense feelings of guilt and shame. The struggle against masturbation fantasies would later be developed theoretically as one of the challenges of the latency process, which help integrate the superego undermined by the onset of puberty. This struggle was also one of the central themes of his later analysis of his daughter Anna (Freud, 1919b), as well as the topic of Anna's first psychoanalytic publication (Freud, 1922).

4.12.3 A young virgin is deflowered

The rest of Freud's paper addresses this transgressive dimension of fantasy: "The most seductive part of the whole subject for a young scapegrace is the picture of the marriage night. (What does he care about what comes afterwards?)" Having been repressed, the fantasy is then replaced by reserve and respect. In addition, the idea "does not develop into a conscious phantasy" but disguises into a *childhood* scene (Freud, 1899, p. 317). This is a curious situation: while from the beginning of the paper, Freud has tried to demonstrate that memories conceal infantile complexes through displacement and condensation, and often in a retrograde direction, in this case the childhood memory appears as if to hide memories of adolescence, reminding us of the reversibility of the memory linked to Freud's bibliophilic tendencies in *The Interpretation of Dreams*. The adolescent material therefore has qualities comparable to the infantile material, in the sense that a repressed sexual conflict also becomes linked to memories of adolescence and is lodged inside a childhood memory. The screen of repression affects both genital and infantile sexuality, while pursuing the historical search for the infantile origins of a disorder. As Freud discovered in 1893, the sexual attacks described by some of his young patients had to do with the profusion of their adolescent fantasies (Freud, 1887–1904). Pubertal sexuality thus comes to the fore of the psychoanalytic discovery, via the development of concepts such as repression and deferred action, and "overt" sexual conflicts. The patient imagined by Freud proceeds in this way when he speaks about the grossly sensual fantasies that "find its way allusively and under a flowery disguise into a childhood scene". This allows Freud to use a sweet childhood memory to show that genital sexuality has become lodged in this "innocent" scene while the adolescent is subject to fantasies of "gross sexual aggression" (p. 317), thus highlighting the specificity and intensity of adolescent sexual fantasies. The connection with the behaviour of hysterical patients is not surprising, given that from the beginning of his career, Freud worked with both young girls (*Madchen*) and boys (*junger Mann*). This clinical work resulted in, for example, the discovery of deferred action in the case of Emma (Freud, 1895) or, as early as in the 1880s, the development of his theoretical and clinical approach to hysteria, which he published some years later (Freud and Breuer, 1895). Furthermore, he adds that the childhood memory is facilitated by the pleasure of remembering the past, suggesting that the memories of adolescence do not carry this kind of satisfaction.

Let us continue: the patient returns to the idea of a happier life, had he married Gisela or another girl – suggesting a regret as to Freud's marriage to Martha. The conflict is displaced to contrast this wishful fantasy with the "dominant sexual disposition" (Freud, 1899, p. 317).

The conscious version was "got rid of" by the changes in the patient's real personal situation; thanks to the innocence of the childhood scene, the repressed idea finds a conscious position in psychic life by "unjustifiably smuggling itself in" among his childhood memories. The link between bread and "bread-and-butter education" connects the infantile and adolescent material through an association that does not simply reproduce the infantile complex. The latter is modified by the importance given to scholarship, which has to do with the complexities of Freud's position as an adolescent. An ascetic with a passion for books and prone to daydreaming, he later wrote (Freud, 1873–1939) that his main sources of satisfaction were to do with the pleasures of imagination and work. The childhood memory conceals forbidden desires and therefore becomes the psychic site where adolescent conflicts are deposited. Freud speaks about the "motives that led to my producing the dandelion phantasy" (Freud, 1899, p. 318), raising questions as to the memory's authenticity. This results in another change in perspective: childhood memories can throw light on adolescent conflicts, which does not put in doubt the infantile roots of psychic life. The innocence of childhood memories acts as a protective screen against the unpleasant and consuming nature of adolescent conflict, represented here by two powerful sources: a desire for material well-being and the desire to deflower. While the latter refers to a sadistic fantasy linked to the violence of sexual desire, the material situation can be seen as a regret, something akin to: "If only I had made a financially happier marriage!"

These desires are strongly repressed and transformed, because they provoke guilt and shame; they are "smuggled in" because of their transgressive and violent nature, or their nostalgia for a missed opportunity. If we step away from Freud's own situation, the fantasy of rape – or indeed a double rape of Pauline, with John, which also includes a homosexual dimension – can be thought of as typical of sadistic sexuality, active for the teenage boy and passive for the girl.

Connected to the interpretation of the dream, the screen-memory is associated with a scene of infantile masturbatory seduction involving the presence of another person, "whereas his seduction to masturbate must have occurred in solitude and secrecy" (Ibid., p. 319). Seeing many strangers in a dream represents a repressed desire to masturbate; the German expression "to pull one out" is a vulgar reference to masturbation; this expression is present in *The Interpretation of Dreams* and refers essentially to the act of pulling out teeth. Freud writes that this interpretation of dreams about teeth being pulled out had always met with strong resistance among his patients, until he discovered an "explanation" that seemed self-evident: "In males the motive force of these dreams was derived from nothing other than the masturbatory desires of the pubertal period" (Freud, 1900, p. 385). He illustrates this with a case of a young gay man, sexually inhibited and a virgin, who imagines sex with men "on the model of the pubertal masturbation with which he had once been familiar" (Ibid., p. 387).

While Freud himself addresses the link between masturbation and the act of pulling out teeth using a memory from his childhood, it is essentially the adolescent material that is emphasised here. The connection with the expression "to pull one out" leads him to introduce Jung's idea that, when occurring in women, dreams with a dental stimulus have the meaning of giving birth, thus introducing the opposition between adolescent feminine and masculine dream significations. When Jung explores the idea of an equivalence between childbirth in women and the loss of a tooth associated with ejaculations in dreams, a case reported by Rank features a toothache again connected to pubertal sexuality. Freud (1913) also linked the knocking out of teeth with an adolescent rite of passage in primitive tribes.

The abundance of material linked to adolescence and masturbation is explicit in the paper on the screen-memories; is masturbating in solitude and secrecy the

characteristic of the polymorphously perverse child who takes pleasure in exhibi-
tionism, or of the adolescent? The memory becomes a screen when it is related,
as Freud does in *The Interpretation of Dreams*, to a childhood memory; it conceals the shame of masturbation and its accompanying fantasies and alludes to
another function of the screen-memory, as a defence against adolescent fantasies
that magnify those of the child no longer protected by his innocence. This loss
of innocence indeed marks one of the most significant differences between the
child and the youth: what is banal or indeed amusing in an inconspicuous child
becomes crude and violent in the psychic life of an adolescent. The Freudian
vocabulary suggests a shift, from infantile innocence to adolescent transgression.

I have already mentioned the central role played by Freud's friend Eduard
Silberstein in his adolescence; I will now return to it in more detail in order to
explore the different facets of this important relationship.

Note

1 I have borrowed this beautiful title from Huber (2009).

Bibliography

Anzieu D. (1959), *L'auto-analyse de Freud*, Paris, PUF.
Bernfeld S. (1951), Sigmund Freud, M. D., 1882–1885, *International Journal of the Psychoanalysis*, 32, p. 204–217.
Bertin C. (2010), *La dernière Bonaparte*, Paris, Perrin.
Boehlich W. (1990), Introduction, in Freud S. (ed.), *Lettres de jeunesse*, Paris, Gallimard, p. 17–31.
Börne L. (1823, 2013), *Die Kunst in drei Tagen ein original Schriftsteller zu werden*, Berlin, Hubert W. Holzinger-Verlag.
Clark R. W. (1985), *Freud, the Man and the Cause*, London, Jonathan Cape and Weiden-feld & Nicolson.
Eissler K. R. (1974), Über Freuds Freundschaft mit Wilhelm Fließ nebst einem Anhang über Freuds Adoleszenz und einer historischen Bemerkung über Freuds Jugendstil, in Eissler K. R. (dir.), *Aus Freuds Sprachwelt und andere Beiträge*, 2, Bern Stuttgart Wien, Verlag Hans Huber, Jahrbuch der Psychoanalyse, p. 39–100.
Eissler K. R. (1978), Creativity and adolescence: the effect of trauma in Freud's adoles-cence, *The Psychoanalytic Study of the Child*, 33, p. 461–518.
Eissler K. R. (2006), Esquisse biographique, in Eissler K., Freud E., Freud L., Grubitch Simitis I., Fleckhaus W. (dir.), *Sigmund Freud. Lieux, visages, objets*, Paris, Gallimard, p. 10–38.
Freud A. (1922, 1994), Fantasme d'être battu et rêverie, in Hamon M. (dir.), *Féminité mascarade*, Paris, Seuil, p. 57–75.
Freud S. (1871–1881, 1990), *Lettres de jeunesse*, Paris, Gallimard.
Freud S. (1895, 1956), *La naissance de la psychanalyse*, Paris, PUF.
Freud S. (1899), *Screen Memories*. SE 3, London, Hogarth Press, p. 299–322.
Freud S. (ed.). (1900), *The Interpretation of Dreams*. SE 4, London, Hogarth Press, p. ix–627.

Freud S. (1901), *The Psychopathology of Everyday Life: Forgetting, Slips of the Tongue, Bungled Actions, Superstitions and Errors (1901)*. SE 6, London, Hogarth Press, p. vii–296.

Freud S. (1909), *Notes Upon a Case of Obsessional Neurosis*. SE 10, London, Hogarth Press, p. 151–318.

Freud S. (1913), *Totem and Taboo: Some Points of Agreement between the Mental Lives of Savages and Neurotics (1913 [1912–13])*. SE 13, London, Hogarth Press, p. vii–162.

Freud S. (1914), *On Narcissism: An Introduction*. SE 14, London, Hogarth Press, p. 67–102.

Freud S. (1916, 1979), *Introduction à la psychanalyse*, Paris, Payot.

Freud S. (1919a), *The 'Uncanny'*. SE 17, London, Hogarth Press, p. 217–256.

Freud S. (1919b), *'A Child is Being Beaten' A Contribution to the Study of the Origin of Sexual Perversions*. SE 17, London, Hogarth Press, p. 175–204.

Freud S. (1925), *An Autobiographical Study*. SE 20, London, Hogarth Press, p. 1–70.

Freud S. (1930), *Civilization and Its Discontents*. SE 2, London, Hogarth Press, p. 57–146.

Freud S. (1979), *Correspondance (1873–1939)*, Paris, Gallimard.

Freud S. (1986), *The Complete Letters to Wilhelm Fliess (1887–1904)*, Cambridge, MA, Harvard University Press.

Freud S. (1990), *Lettres de jeunesse (1871–1881)*, Paris, Gallimard.

Freud S., Breuer J. (1895), *Studies on Hysteria*. SE 2, London, Hogarth Press, p. ix–310.

Gallo R. (2009), Freud's Spanish: binlinguism and bisexuality, *Psychoanalysis and History*, 11, p. 5–40.

Gay P. (1991), *Freud: A Life for Our Time*, New York, W.W. Norton & Co.

Grubrich-Simitis I. (1925, 1984), Introduction, in Freud S. (ed.), *Ma vie et la psychanalyse. Contribution à l'histoire de la psychanalyse*, Paris, Gallimard, p. 7–33.

Hamilton J. W. (2002), Freud and the suicide of Pauline Silberstein, *Psychoanalytic Review*, 89, p. 889–909.

Houssier F. (2010), *L'école d'Anna Freud. Créativité et controverses*, Paris, Editions Campagne Première.

Houssier F. (2013), *Meurtres dans la famille*, Paris, Dunod.

Houssier F. (2016), Entre S. Freud et S. Ferenczi, un Œdipe pubertaire?, *Les lettres de la SPF*, 35, p. 157–173.

Huber G. (2009), *Si c'était Freud*, Lormond, Le bord de l'eau.

Jones E. (1958, 2006), *La vie et l'œuvre de S. Freud, T. 1: La jeunesse de Freud (1856–1900)*, Paris, PUF.

Krüll M. (1979), *Sigmund, fils de Jacob*, Paris, Gallimard.

Rocah B. S. (2002), The language of flowers: Freud's adolescent language of love, lust and longing, *The Psychoanalytic Study of the Child*, 57, p. 377–399.

Rodrigué E. (2000), *Freud. Le siècle de la psychanalyse*, Paris, Payot, T. 1.

Roudinesco E. (2014), *Freud: In his Time and Ours*, Cambridge, MA, Harvard University Press.

Schacht L. (2006), L'inclination a fait son apparition comme un beau jour de printemps . . ., *Revue Française de Psychanalyse*, 70(1), p. 215–228.

Stanescu H. (1965), Unbekannte Briefe des jungen Freud an einen rumänischen Freund, *Neue Literatur*, 16, p. 123–129.

Eduard

The passion of friendship

Freud's correspondence with Eduard Silberstein is key to understanding the sharp edges of Freud's teenage years. Contrary to the openly biographical psychoanalytical texts in which Freud returns to his own past, often fragmentarily and at times deliberately transforming it, his nearly decade-long correspondence with Silberstein is concomitant with this period of his life. Though they have been commented on by a number of authors, the relatively recent discovery of their letters has meant that they have not been analysed systematically as a whole, which I will attempt to do in this chapter.

5.1 An overview

Freud's friendship with Eduard Silberstein (1856–1925) left a profound mark on his life. In 1884, he wrote to Silberstein's fiancée that they became close at a time when friendship was not a kind of sport or advantage, but a vital need. In the light of Freud's complaint that his school did not sufficiently prepare its students for the separation from their families, on reading these letters we see clearly that the process of detaching himself from the protective figures of his childhood was one of the most painful tasks of Freud's life, as he would later put it in his key text on adolescence (Freud, 1905). The tumultuous relationship with his best friend can therefore be read as a story of conflict between, on the one hand, a search for a double and, on the other hand, a separation that involved the challenges of individuation and personalisation (Houssier, 2014) in trying to create a life as an adult.

5.1.1 Friendship as a vital need

We do not know when exactly their friendship began, but their families had been friendly already in Freiberg and the two boys were meeting regularly as early as in 1870. While middle school has been cited as a possible meeting place, Boehlich also speaks of the role played by their mothers. Amalia Freud, whose health was rather delicate, often went to the spa in Roznau near Freiberg, usually accompanied by one or several of her children. Freud thus speaks about his mother in a

DOI: 10.4324/9781003340898-5

letter to Silberstein, telling him she has been suffering from a pulmonary disease that has kept her bedridden and is planning to have a treatment in Roznau. It is possible that as early as in 1869, Freud made the journey with his mother, meeting up with Anna Silberstein and her son Eduard. This hypothesis brings into play the friendship established between the mothers and, as its echo, the two teenage boys.

Their correspondence initially started during a summer holiday not spent together and continued throughout the year, given their respective trajectories, eventually spanning an entire decade (Freud, 1871–1881). After his school-leaving exam, Silberstein left for Leipzig to study law. He later returned to Vienna and in 1875 started attending the lectures of the renowned philosopher Franz Brentano.

Among the friends of Freud's youth, I have already mentioned Heinrich Braun, Emil Fluss and Wilhelm Knöpfmacher; we should also include Richard Whale, Joseph Paneth, Emanuel Löwy, Horaz Ignaz Rosanes, Joseph Bettelheim, Jacob Theumann, someone called Brust, a friend from university and a colleague, and Konrad Löw. Those closest to Eduard were Luess, Herzig, K. F. Grön, Léopold Herzog and Anton Reitler (Heim, 1990), whom Freud cites in a postscript to the letter of 22–23rd October 1874 to Eduard. Reitler joined the Wednesday society in 1902. Except for his relatively close friendship with Braun, nobody held as important a place in Freud's life as Eduard. His other teenage friendships, for example with Joseph Paneth, lasted for a certain time, but we have little to go on as to the role they played in young Freud's life.

Still, we should mention Rosanes, who appears in the correspondence with Silberstein and was originally Freud's classmate. Rosanes became the director of the Kronprinzessin Stephanie Hospital in Vienna and together with Freud assisted Wilhelm Fliess during Emma Eckstein's surgery. Or Emanuel Löwy, who studied classical archaeology in Vienna and became a professor of archaeology and art history at the University of Rome. Löwy had a great influence over Freud, who defined psychoanalysis as the "archaeology of the soul" precisely following discussions with Löwy and reading his works. To support this hypothesis, note that Freud wrote to Fliess that Löwy came to see him once every year and they would stay up talking until three in the morning.

Eduard's father, also of Jewish origin, settled in Braila, on the Danube, to start a business and send his children to study in Vienna. Political instability, the plague, cholera and anti-Jewish pogroms had forced him out of Eduard's native town of Jassy in Romania. He wanted to raise his children in a strictly orthodox Talmudic tradition, but eventually gave in to their resistance. Eduard revolted against the rigid and constricting aspects of his education, so much so that he and his brother left the Jewish school where their father had enrolled them. Freud once described Eduard's father, a banker by profession, as "half mad".

The friendship resulted in a rich correspondence (Freud, 1871–1881), of which we only have Freud's own eighty letters. His friends' missives no doubt burnt in the 1895 auto-da-fé (Heim, 1990), thus polishing Freud's own portrait rather than Silberstein's. This is not without importance; when he writes to his fiancée that he decided on this first burning of documents while reading a book on Russian history, his tone is triumphant. His biographers would no doubt "resent" his decision (Freud, 1873–1939, p. 140), but, he explains, his past thoughts and feelings about the world in general have been found unworthy of further existence. Everything must be thought anew, especially because the papers piling up around him are like the sand drifts round the Sphinx, and soon nothing but his nostrils will be visible. "I couldn't have matured or died without worrying about who would get hold of those old papers", he adds.

All that belongs to the past before his life's great turning point, that is, their love and his choice of profession, has long been dead and deserves a worthy funeral – and let the biographers worry about their errors as to the "Development of the Hero". This shame of his boyhood makes this auto-da-fé a rite of passage, spelling the end of his adolescence, as we shall later see.

Paradoxically, while Freud's intention in burning the documents was to thwart his biographers, the effect of discovering these letters was precisely the opposite. They reveal not just his quick wit and humour, but show a man passionate about science, making precise and occasionally bold claims. He defines himself as an atheist or even an anti-religious materialist, sharing with his friend his Jewish culture and ideas of female emancipation, which he at times contradicts. The letters abound with intellectual influences that informed his entire life's work (the list would be too long), from Schiller to Goethe and including Feuerbach and Shakespeare.

5.1.2 Founding a royal academy

Boehlich (1990) suggests that no one played as important a role in Freud's teenage years as Silberstein and that Freud never forgot their times together. The creation of the *Academia Castellana* was a shared fantasy of self-engendering: learning Spanish without taking lessons, inventing a private mythology exclusive to the couple and shared via often very funny letters.

Even during his life, few people knew that Freud spoke, wrote and read Spanish, the language of secrets he had shared with Eduard. This specific secret was only divulged on rare occasions, such as the translation of his complete works into Spanish and in a few letters. In February 1934, Freud wrote to a South American disciple, Carranca y Trujillo, that as a young man he had the pleasure of learning this beautiful language and could thus appreciate the article he had received from him. When their correspondence began in 1871, the process of learning Spanish exclusively through reading (Cervantès, C. Böhl de Faber) and the creation of the Spanish academy were already well under way. Though he was never quite comfortable in Spanish, Freud also never completely forgot the language, as attested to by his letter to the Spanish translator of his works. His use of Spanish, without relying on a dictionary, sometimes meant that he invented words, used them out of context, or Hispanised German expressions. Already as a teenager, Freud greatly enjoyed playing with language.

He started learning Spanish at fifteen; it is not clear how: without a teacher and together with Eduard. The fantasy of self-teaching represents more precisely a symbolic parricide tainted with self-generation. Their secret society had an impressive administrative structure (Gallo, 2009). They wrote down its laws, articles, rules and official documents; there was a wax stamp with the initials "A. C." to mark their correspondence (Eissler et al., 2006). The Academy had a seal; before calling it the Spanish Academy, they had used the abbreviation "SSS" for *Spanisch-Sprache-Schule* (Spanish Language School). Just like for the Hietzing School founded by his daughter Anna in 1927 (Houssier, 2010), a seal was thus created for the *Academia Castellana*, a royal crown above two letters, A and C.

We learned Spanish together, had our own mythology and secret names, which we took from some dialogue of the great Cervantes. [. . .] Together we founded a strange scholarly society, the "Academia Castellana" (AC), compiled a great mass of humorous work which must still exist somewhere among my old papers; we shared our frugal suppers and were never bored in each other's company,

Freud wrote to Martha in February 1884, before burning these documents (Freud, 1873–1939, p. 96).

Freud was thus playing with German and Spanish, improvising between the languages to create a curious patois, a code which the two boys alone could understand. He spared no occasion to complexify this code: for instance, the members of the Academy could never say that someone had died, but rather that he or she had "left Sevilla". In this newspeak, typical of the intimate space teenagers tend to build together with their "double", each life or death had to take on Hispanic inflections, carefully masking the central question. The theme of death had to be enveloped, by inventing a distraction or a metaphorical avoidance formula to lessen the impact of the fantasy, which was either murderous or related to the loss of a loved one.

I have already highlighted the quasi-amorous intensity of this passionate friendship. In August 1873, Freud speaks for the first time about sending Eduard a picture; he sends one in January 1875, a photo of himself with a poem written on the back. He would ask Eduard to send one in return five times. According to Roudinesco, the "dialogues of the dogs" with Silberstein were later replaced by the "congresses" with Wilhelm Fliess: "They came to see each other as twin brothers and had their picture taken with the same beards, the same clothes, and the same look; they distributed this portrait to their friends" (Roudinesco, 2016, p. 55). Other authors such as Hamilton (2002) or Gedo and Wolf (1976) also highlight the mirrorlike proximity between the two.

The Academy represented a shared space, made up of clever tricks, containing and protecting the boys' fantasies and confidences; but it was also the couple's child, where in Freud's own words they were united by the bonds of marriage and the shared future of the Academy.

Freud's criticisms and sermonising apropos Eduard's alleged frivolity with girls resonated with this imaginary adage: better to suffer the moralism of a harsh superego than risk the strange and dangerous encounter with female sexuality (Gallo, 2009). It is thus no surprise that in this context, Freud's letters to his friend also contained feelings of insecurity, jealousy and painful self-doubt.

5.1.3 A terrible tale: the witch's terrifying sexuality

The context for the letters was the creation of a learned society, its two members relying on a shared literary reference, Cervantes' novella *The Dialogue of the Dogs* (2009). Each of them adopted the name of one of the main characters: Freud became "Cipion, the dog of the Sevilla Hospital" and Silberstein took on the character of "Berganza".

In the novella, a man is duped out of his possessions by a prostitute and is eventually hospitalised. In the hospital, he sees two dogs who begin to speak at the stroke of midnight. They talk about their masters and the different places they have lived. The dialogue questions the relationship between fantasy and reality, with Cervantes letting the reader decide whether the dogs are indeed talking, or the hero is simply hallucinating. For the boys, the two languages, Spanish and German, also stood for the opposition between reality and fantasy. In this respect, we are reminded of Cervantes' other famous character, Don Quixote, or the tales of E.T.A. Hoffman (Freud, 1919). We do not know where or how Freud came across the novella, but we can assume he identified with the more active and dominant or didactic of the two dogs, Cipion. Looking at their dialogue, the relationship between the two dogs resembles the analytical setting; Grinberg and Rodriguez (1984) speak about a psychoanalytical atmosphere, where Berganza speaks freely about his traumas, misfortunes and personal details, but also the confusion between his feelings, thoughts and dreams, while Cipion is listening, trying to understand and counsel. The two authors argue that Freud felt guilty for learning Spanish, because it distracted him from his everyday tasks and studies. Gedo and Wolf (1976) see his interest in Cervantes as a way of identifying with a great man, which continued throughout Freud's adolescence, a quixotic dream of being *someone* – a writer – and later conquer the world through psychoanalysis. Like Cervantes, Freud was fond of military heroes and would transform them into protagonists able to defeat the enemy through words. Like Freud's conversations with Eduard, the dialogue of the two dogs was set in a purely masculine world; any female Berganza mentions turns out to be corrupt, lying or dishonest. On appearance, each woman seems pretty, but in fact proves to be licentious, a prostitute, blackmailing a corrupt policeman or stealing money from foreigners. And yet, the worst is still to come; towards the end of the story, Berganza meets an old witch, Canizares, who lures him into her house with the promise to tell him about this birth. She reveals to him that he is in fact a human being, transformed into a dog by an evil spell. She wants to kiss him on the mouth, but Berganza rejects her, which Cipion approves of by saying that being kissed by an old woman is torture rather than pleasure. To undo the spell, the witch performs a strange ritual, which requires her to undress and rub her body with a mysterious ointment. Faced with this naked body, Berganza panics. He is still terrified, as he is describing her body to Cipion: she is seven feet tall, a bag of bones covered in dark, hairy and tanned hide. She has a stomach like a sheepskin, covering her genitals, hanging down to her thighs. Her breasts are a dry cow's udders; her lips and teeth are black, her nose crooked and deformed, her eyes wild and hair scruffy, and so on. This trauma drives Berganza to bite her, his revulsion so strong that he eventually attacks her in the most sadistic scene of the story, gripping her stomach and dragging her across the yard as she is screaming for help, begging to be saved from the jaws of this evil spirit.

In the novella, which like many fairy tales features a witch, the intimate and platonic exchange between the two dogs is haunted by the spectre of women, who are portrayed as deceitful, confusing and physically terrifying. The last female character, a tiny female dog, is the object of a sadistic fantasy – being ignored or torn into shreds by Berganza's teeth. In the story, men speak to improve themselves through conversation; women only speak to seduce, deceive or traumatise men, alluding to the horror of female sexuality and incest. The female body is monstrous; its dry breasts have no milk. The witch represents the primordial mother, seductive and devouring her children.

Gedo and Wolf argued that Cervantes' text had an autobiographical meaning reflecting the inner conflicts of young Freud and helping him become conscious of them without having to live them. Freud entered his teenage years yearning for figures of identification and initially looked towards writers such as Cervantes for a parental ideal. Identifying with the author's humour and his grandiose self-image also his quixotic tendencies with Gisela.

In *The Dialogue of the Dogs*, Freud also found the literary device of creating a fictional dialogue to express different perspectives on a subject, which he would later use, for example, in the paper on the screen-memories (Freud, 1899). As a young boy, he borrowed his style from the Latin poet Horacio and went through a series of identifications with other great authors such as Shakespeare and Goethe, whom he began to read already at the age of eight. Cervantes appears more specific to his teenage hero identifications.

Spanish was the language of doubt, of emotional ambivalence and the ill-defined teenage sexual identity, as well as the language of affective intensity, a Pandora's box which, after his friendship with Eduard had faded, Freud mostly kept closed. It eventually returned in his correspondence with Ferenczi (Houssier, 2016), to whom he addressed the ultimate expression of teenage uncertainty: *Quien sabe?*

5.1.4 First writings on unconscious searching

Without exaggeration, it is difficult to read these letters and not think about their points of resonance with Freud's future creation of psychoanalysis. For example, they highlight his interest in "unconscious searching" or his belief that "youthful impressions are hard to obliterate" (Freud, 1871–1881, p. 89, 118), which can be added to, for example, the oedipal "transference" of Freud's love for Gisela to her mother.

While Eduard tried to raise Freud's awareness of socio-democratic politics, the latter was not particularly keen and at times criticised his friend's activism, ostensibly preferring the realm of ideas. As Roudinesco and Plon (1997) suggest, one of the drivers of their debates was a wish to use intellect to surpass their respective fathers and their professional aspirations. Freud imagined becoming a philosopher and Silberstein wanted to work as a lawyer. The reference to Cervantes, who so well describes the fact of mistaking oneself for another, is therefore not accidental; the relationship of substitution, of making the other one's double, is typical of the passionate friendships of adolescence. Starting from the first psychoanalytical studies of adolescence, a transitory homosexuality and its sublimation were considered a psychic necessity of puberty, binding young people to one another and helping them create a sense of identity (Freud, 1905; Bernfeld, 1922).

The letters also remind us that in one of the first leading theoretical texts on adolescence, Bernfeld (Ibid., p. 65) speaks about "genius adolescence", specifically the creation of imaginary societies. In his article, the author, whom Freud greatly admired, illustrates the teenage investment of cultural objects and ideals by a case study of two seventeen-year-olds who created a society with a humanitarian mission, which they called a "Free Society of Those Becoming" (p. 58). This awareness of teenagerhood as a process is also present in Freud's writing, for example, in explaining to Eduard what a student's life should be, as we shall see later. As Bernfeld concludes, adolescence is not only an encounter with the opposite sex but also the discovery of oneself, a narcissistic affirmation of the need for uniqueness and difference from others. Or, we could add, a search for one's double and then a gradual detachment, highlighting the challenges of subjective construction that are characteristic of adolescence and to which these letters frequently attest.

In the final year of their correspondence, Freud's writing became less passionate, less romantic, playful or intimate. He learnt to sublimate his feelings, taking a more serious approach to his studies. Eduard's decision to return to Romania and work in the family business was a disappointment to Freud, who had great intellectual ambitions for his friend. Even after the end of their relationship, he continued to express a certain hostility towards Eduard's girlfriends.

5.1.5 Blood relations

Freud's constant preoccupation with keeping their confidences secret also applied to his relationships with young girls or women. When speaking sincerely, he seems to have been more comfortable maintaining a platonic admiration for a young girl, Gisela, with whom nothing could really happen, than to assert his sensual desires for her. He forbade himself looking at beautiful women – even just looking would be too intense – and when he *did* look, he would compare them to prostitutes. Thus, he protected himself from the sight of women by "rendering them untouchable", Boehlich writes (1990, p. 26). His phobic position was equally apparent when he would try to keep his friend on the straight and narrow: before Eduard's supposedly loose morals, Freud behaved as part psychologist, part educator, urging his friend to exercise more restraint. He used the arguments of precisely the kind of bourgeois morality his later work would continuously disprove and link to the origins of neurosis.

His humour sometimes tempered and attenuated the intensity of his emotional demands on his friend, which were at times made quite concretely, such as in telling him off for being slow to respond. He tried to get involved in all of Eduard's affairs, reproached him for not writing regularly and questioned his affection for him. The greed with which he awaited each letter or package would at times make him seem both tyrannical and dependent.

This double relation was characteristic of all Freud's passionate friendships and found its direct echo in his later relationship with Wilhelm Fliess. His words illustrate the twin-like friendships of adolescence: "We 'take the road' shoulder to shoulder and 'bras dessus, bras dessous' [arm in arm]" (Freud, 1871–1881, p. 45). His sexual abstinence as a teenager evokes the asceticism sustained by over-intellectualisation also found in his youngest daughter Anna, who later identified these two elements as key modes of defence against the potentially overwhelming power of adolescent drives (Freud, 1936; Houssier, 2010).

Looking at Freud's personality at the time, we may wonder about the long-term effects of this abstinence, which later found its theoretical equivalent in his notion of the actual neurosis (Freud, 1898). It was anchored in an ideal, his sense of vocation, which first emerged as a daydream, of having a laboratory and enough free time, or having a ship on the ocean with all the researcher's tools. In this context, he names England as a place that could offer such working conditions as to "strike out on new therapeutical paths" (Freud, 1871–1881, p. 127).

This solitary Freud who rejects the kind of sexual freedom claimed by his friend also reminds us of the sailors who, as he would later write, would engage in homosexual acts due to the absence of women. It is impossible not see a form of jealousy here, which is at least twofold: Silberstein has relationships with young women – and this also means he abandons Freud. This is corroborated by Freud's nearly continuous love declarations, for instance when he writes: "We are as attached to one another as if nature had put [us] on this earth as blood relations" (Ibid., p. 126).

This blood relation appears here in a fraternal homosexual form; was this not the situation of the older brothers of the primitive horde, banished by their father? In Freud's myth (Freud, 1913, 1915), these young men then found themselves as if forced into homosexuality, no doubt a powerful motive to return and kill the father, who caused this regression by denying them access to women (Houssier, 2013a).

5.2 Writing one's feelings

Let's now look in more detail at Freud's language in these letters. In doing so, we will try to represent the young man's journey in terms of his use of language, given his unusual ability to combine metapsychology and literary style.

5.2.1 The pure gold of language

The letters give us a glimpse into Freud's frame of mind and emotional state. His changing moods are apparent in the sudden breaks or at-times contradictory alternations in tone. The defensive trivialisation of the "principles" – one day we will laugh about this, it is not worth talking about, and so on – sits alongside the idea that life might be "one of the strangest things in the world" (Freud, 1871–1881, p. 12). These dysphoric oscillations are combined with sudden changes of subject, using a style that is already highly associative.

Some passages help us understand the contents of Eduard's letters. Freud protests being called "gloomy and sad" by Eduard, when in fact he feels "more light-hearted than ever". It is mostly in "unguarded moments" that his forlorn mood invades him, sign of an intense struggle involving a manic defence, but also attesting to the withdrawal of libidinal investments from his first love-objects.

Freud's style is deliberately ironic, elegant, precise, passionate and persuasive. For example, the discussion about the "principles" is part of the musicality of his style; when he talks about Eduard friend's Löw's "celebrated love", he highlights the contrast between how the girl had been described to him by Eduard and what he saw himself: "I expected to see a heroic and vengeful maid and what I found was a plain, plump, and cheerful girl" (Ibid., p. 4). The difference between the image of an idealised conquering maid and the reality of the young girl is disappointing: Freud adds that she does not compare to "Ichth", who thus appears in their correspondence for the first time. This reference to Freud's love interest, who in this case is not necessarily Gisela Fluss, is equally a source of disappointment: he saw his brother and not her, or he complains of not having seen her for two weeks. At this time, during the summer of 1872, Freud reproaches his friend for pretending to have been the first one to kiss a girl. By pointing out his contradictions, a first hint of suspicion appears, when he asks Eduard if he is mocking him. Yet he also says about the kiss: "How well off you are!" and signs off as "Your unfortunate Cipion", alluding to the absence of his own love interest.

Over time, his impatience and demands for Eduard's letters became more pressing. In the letter dated 9th August 1872, Freud complains that a week has gone by without a response from Eduard and decries his friend's fickleness. While rationally he dismisses the idea that this silence might preoccupy him, he only alludes to Eduard's neglect and adds: "I cannot help thinking that you may have been stricken by something" (Ibid., p. 9). The hard-to-suppress aggressiveness takes the shape of an anxious fantasy and can be more easily expressed as a joke, when Freud writes that what interests him now is knowing whether "Your Honour" has gone to hell or not.

Freud could be sarcastic or even vengeful when his friend appeared unreliable and did not write as often as promised. When he ironically informs Eduard about his day-to-day by describing his various outings – he is missing Eduard, makes it clear to him and cannot easily tolerate his friend's potential indifference – he says he wrote two Spanish lines on a table of an inn, signing them "D. Berganza" to "perpetuate your name".

The trip is to the village of Hochwald, which Freud describes as a "paradise". The pain of Eduard's absence is accentuated by his idealised portrayal of the ruined castle, so full of history. Substituting himself for his friend is a way of pretending the moment was shared by them, as if their identity was interchangeable, one writing for the other. The letter ends on a promise: he will write as soon as he hears Eduard is alive but is expecting valuable and copious letters in return. The following letter, written eight days later, begins with an apology as to this accusation of negligence: "I hope you will forgive my impatience" (Ibid., p. 10). He then explains he has started a diary to share with his dearly missed friend.

What Freud saw as an imbalance in their relationship – Eduard kept his thoughts to himself while Freud tended to overshare – was linked to his barely concealed demand for exclusivity. "I hope that your telling of them will more than make up for this", he writes. However, this does not prevent him pining for his friend, evoking their quasi-romantic "evening saunters and nocturnal visits". Freud is feeling the pain of this absence and comparing Eduard to another friend, Rosanes, who is a poor listener. This unsatisfied "need for communication" has put him in a bad mood. Yet he is also surprised: over the preceding days, he has written with such frankness in his letter to Eduard that he could well be writing in his diary. His need for reciprocity in conversation combines with a hope that no one else may read their letters; these intimate "confessions" might be made easier by their habitual use of Spanish (Ibid., p. 11).

5.2.2 Matters of the heart

The following letter, sent from Freiberg on 4th September 1872, carries on this demand for reciprocity in their friendship. Freud wonders if he can forgive his friend for saying so little in his last letter, while recognising that he cannot ask for more than Eduard is willing to give. The writing of the diary and the letters resonate with Freud's dream-interpretation in his correspondence with Fliess, which too helped him identify his insights and establish an associative mode of thinking. Writing from his hometown, Freud imagines that Eduard feels the same about their separation, of being "suddenly torn out of your familiar and beloved circle" (Ibid., p. 14). The fact of not being particularly busy makes "the pain of your loss" even stronger. Freud is staying with the Flusses, while Eduard is in Braila. His inability to laugh at Gisela, which he confides in Eduard, is underpinned by an anxiety, namely that Eduard might tell Rosanes or someone else, who might indeed mock him. The fear of being "laughable" or "ridiculous" highlights the seriousness of the subject and Freud's own narcissistic sensitivity. Contrary to the praise lavished on Emil, Freud shows no affection towards Rosanes, who has "no feeling for frankness or purity" (Ibid., p. 16). By contrast, his description paints Freud's own self-portrait: a respectful, generous idealist, but also a demanding and tyrannical moralist. Rosanes is said to have never understood Freud and Eduard's bond, highlighting the exclusion of anyone at odds with the nature of their friendship. The relationship with Rosanes, with whom it seems Freud nevertheless got on very well, despite the lack of any deep understanding between them, implicitly contrasts with the connection between Freud and Eduard, their "hearts' affections" (Ibid.), with Freud often imagining Eduard in Rosanes' place.

While he is worried about the precise date of Eduard's arrival and their separation during the academic year, he again writes to Eduard: "Then we shall continue our secret studies with renewed strength and forge a new bond." Do these secret studies concern the "principles" or their Spanish academy? The fact remains that it is Freud who takes initiative, feverishly waiting for this friendship to resume and relying on its emotional sustenance just as he feels weaned off it. The new bond he is calling for requires more exclusivity: his impatience and impetuousness reveal the intensity of his feelings, when he demands his last letter to be answered immediately, concluding: "In that case your obdurate heart and indurate mouth might open up to let me know that you are not yet dead to me" (Ibid., p. 19).

5.2.3 Alter ego or double?

What Freud wants is a new and more exclusive bond; he is bored of spending his evenings strolling with others, and even says that he and Eduard can "dispense with a third for an audience". The postscript shows that Eduard also committed a bungled action when he signed his letter dated 2nd June 1875 "Cipion". Jokingly, Freud pretends to be offended by this misappropriation; then suggests that they could trade names, if Eduard so wishes.

Freud again weaves together a kind of confusion between them, or a substitution of one for the other, in instructing his friend: "Do on your own what we should do if we were together: walk, toy with your thoughts, drink water from the springs, and gather strawberries in the fields" (Ibid., p. 21), attesting to his close carnal link between physical activity and a contact with nature.

He describes his rambles, talks about girding his loins and seizing a stick, about his galloping stride. His letters to Eduard from 16th and 17th July 1873 bring a new fantasy substitution: Freud transmits his powers so that his friend may eat what they would otherwise have eaten together. The conflict between his inactivity, which he sees as a form of laziness, and his desire to work towards success, already appears as a criticism of this presumed indolence. However, he warns against nostalgia: "Finding the past beautiful is pure luxury in most cases" (Ibid., p. 23), and he must instead focus on his future success.

In August 1873, Freud says, citing Goethe, that a man must be himself, as he wishes to be. Regarding his own pleasures, he writes: "Get up into the mountains by yourself and let books and society rot. Get into the mountains, I say, and eat strawberries. Eat strawberries, I say, and forget you are by yourself" (Ibid., p. 32).

This romantic tirade is deeply ambivalent: on the one hand, an ascetic overvaluing of the world of books, on the other, a rejection of this intellectual overinvestment in favour of the libidinal enjoyment of the body and nature. It also makes space for intense nostalgia, a homesickness for the place where Eduard is staying, close to Freiberg. It is a twofold nostalgia: alongside Freud's relationship with his father, whose hand he would be holding on his first walks in the woods, it also connects to the maternal world. The walks and enjoyment of nature are very present in these letters: the river, meadows, plants and trees make up the décor of these bucolic rambles. The comparison between the landscape around Freiberg and the outskirts of Vienna fuels Freud's ambivalence towards the latter. He asks Eduard to go to the meadowland "opposite the house in which my mother stayed last year" (Ibid., p. 33), look for the fragrant twigs of a thuja or a cypress tree, and send him a sample. His nostalgia for the maternal world from which he was so brutally torn away is palpable here, strengthening his ambivalence vis-à-vis his lacking father. During this time, Eduard is staying with Freud's mother and siblings in Roznau and the comparison between the two natural environments is highly unfavourable to "ridiculous" Vienna. Since Eduard's departure from Vienna, Freud has already gone mountaineering four times, adding that "My heart is in the Highlands" (Ibid.).

Walking, eating and drinking were ways of repressing not just young Freud's investment of intellectual life but also his deep feelings of solitude. His ambition had little tolerance for idleness and relaxation, and instead unfolded primarily in his intense passion for books. This was likely part of the anti-cathexis of the body, in favour of the bodily metaphors that abound in his letters and his later work. In the late summer of 1873, Freud thanks Eduard for helping his mother and sisters prepare for their return to Vienna; he makes plans for their reunion, especially "talking, walking, driving about" (Ibid., p. 44), or again taking the road "shoulder to shoulder" (Ibid.). He concludes: "I await you with longing", hinting at the incandescence of the drives that assail him. On the contrary, when again he mentions Rosanes, who has also been away, he says: "Revolutions are occurring in him, too, but of a liquid sort, not fiery as with us" (Ibid., p. 29), as a way of describing how adolescence is at work between them. While Rosanes' revolutions are lukewarm water, Freud's friendship with Eduard is made of fire and the burning desires they share.

5.2.4 A house for two

Freud's passionate attachment to Silberstein was regularly interspersed with moments of intense identification with his friend, provoking an oscillation between discovering an alter ego, an auxiliary ego that left room for a certain degree of alterity, and a double, that is, a narcissistic projection with little space for otherness (Houssier, 2013b). This vacillation helps us understand Freud's occasional tyrannical or authoritarian outbursts. Freud struggled with their separations when his friend became more independent, especially by flirting with girls.

Freud experienced these moments as a betrayal of their bond, which was founded on closeness with little differentiation. Here is an example of his attempt to revive this highly idealised connection.

The letter that signals the resumption of their correspondence during the following summer, dated 13th August 1874, conveys Freud's wish to create an indefectible relationship, where no separation could be imagined. Like an architect, Freud constructs his letter as a three-storey "house". The first level concerns their friendship and correspondence, and what comes out has to do with Freud's worries about their letters following a precise order, that of a "work of art, whose parts are not merely distinct, but also closely interrelated" (Ibid., p. 48).

The second floor is dedicated to Freud's observations about himself and his works and non-works, as if anticipating his future self-analysis. In this paragraph, he describes his daily life, a sedentary life spent "between two pieces of furniture" (p. 49), his armchair and his desk. He is reading Helmoltz's lectures, Carlyle and Aristotle.

The third floor is written in Spanish, suggesting that it concerns girls; however, rather than proceeding with his usual confidence, Freud's message is not very clear and gets lost in generalities and literary references. Yet a trace emerges that we find again later: after having spent days planning a solitary excursion, in the morning he never dares to predict a beautiful day. Because he cannot believe in his good fortune, he ends up missing out when the weather is in fact gorgeous.

He concludes the letter by speaking to his friend as his double: while he is the master builder of the house, Eduard is its owner and should therefore amble through the floors "at [his] leisure". The archives of their Academy will later be part of another project: to "transmute the six prosaic and unrelenting working days of the week into the pure gold of poetry" (Ibid., p. 58).

That his friend may be the owner of this psychic house for two is part of a series of doubling or splits involving Eduard. When Freud (1919) suddenly saw his image in the mirror, he described his experience of seeing his double, unrecognised as such, as terrifying and unpleasant, an archaic reaction felt against an uncanny double. He connected this uncanny encounter to a time where the ego was not yet separate from the world outside, highlighting an archaic dimension experienced and sometimes pursued by many adolescents.

Let's return to the structure of this virtual house. It suggests a possible hypothesis: the stacked construction is not dissimilar to the different levels of the metapsychological edifice and its architectural metaphoric resonances. The concern with building a whole from parts that are equally critical, while being both distinct and interrelated, cuts through this fantasy of a house for two like the one of the metapsychological witch, who sometimes dons the guise of a fairy.

Freud (Ibid., p. 89) recounts having indulged in an old pleasure, reading the papers of the Academy and revelling in the memories of a time gone by. As if to rid himself of the castrating effects of nostalgia, he writes, for the first time, about his wish to burn his papers: "I wanted to propose an auto-da-fé", he begins, then gives up on the idea, suggesting that the first floor of their house will metaphorically be taken up with the secretariat of the Academy and the preservation of their archives. He notices "with sorrow" the absence of his scientific essay, presumably an ironic one, on "Goethe's mouthparts"; he would be "extremely grateful" if his friend could search for this precious document. At the end he announces the paper has in fact turned up.

The contents of these archives, the documents brought by Eduard's brother, included Freud's letter of sympathy, written entirely in Spanish, when he found out that Eduard must leave for Braila, as well as the visiting cards he used whenever his friend was not at home. There were also programmes for the children's theatre drafted by Freud; extracts from Freuds' sisters' diaries brought by Eduard; a report of his "strange meeting with Icht", which might be an allusion to Gisela (Ibid., p. 90) and which he shared both with Eduard and his journal; finally, a poetic treatise "which alone sufficed to immortalize me as Aristotle's fortunate successor", whose book on *Poetics* he also mentions.

5.2.5 A lost letter

A very worried letter follows the news that Eduard did not receive on time a letter and a package that seem to have gotten lost. Freud stresses that rather than the book or the postage cost, the real loss is the letter, which is irreplaceable. It contained a particular passage, "a biblical study with modern themes", something that he could not write again and of which he felt proud. Rather sweetly, he adds: "It would have refreshed you like balm." The short essay conveyed a feeling "so sensitive, so biblically naive and forceful, so melancholy and so gay", a reflection of his current mental state (p. 26). In the following letter, the theme of his worry is further accentuated: the lost essay was a "a masterpiece of a biblical idyll" (Ibid., p. 27).

Freud is now worried about the reliability of the postal service and wants to know if his sister Dolfi has received the four issues of *Kinderfeste*, penned by the psychiatrist Heinrich Hoffmann, the author of "Struwwelpeter", a series of children's stories he and his daughter later commented on (Freud, 1916; Freud, 1930, Houssier, 2013a). Presumably these illustrated stories were Freud's birthday gift to his sister.

Though he was hoping to finally see his friend, the conclusion to the letter dated 30th July 1973 finds him in a mood "too depressed and uncertain" (Freud, 1871–1881, p. 27), and he complains to Eduard of deadly boredom. On finally receiving an answer, the disastrous loss of his "biblical study", which seems to have disappeared somewhere in Hungary, has left him inconsolable; he compares it to the explosion of the sun and the drying up of the sea (Ibid., p. 33).

He would like to give him the latest news "haphazardly, as they spring to mind" (p. 28), while wondering, warily, to whom his friend has shown his letters. He brings up several allegedly silly thoughts that come to his mind, which he declines to develop unless his mood changes. One of these is probably that "I earnestly pondered the possibility of creating a system of numbers", after having observed that everything in the real world had its counterpart in the world of numbers. While this idea has been linked to the Jewish mystical tradition (Bakan, 1964), we are also reminded of Freud's later readiness to believe in Fliess' theory of vital periodicities. This quasi-magic belief therefore stemmed not just from the intensity of his relationship with Fliess but also from one of these many ideas that "spring to mind". The rest of the letter shows how such idea is received, that is, as a shortcut towards human beings who, like numbers, "are born, die, marry and destroy one another" (Freud, 1871–1881, p. 34). He even includes mythology and gods in the comparison.

Later, he adds: "Needless to say, I await your contributions to my numbers system", showing that he could not accept their different desires and positions, and would regularly urge his friend to do the same as him. Moreover, this expectation again anticipated the later relationship with Fliess and some others. In order to formulate his own ideas and, perhaps especially, to encourage his associative capacities, he needed a close friend to support him, recognise his talents and stimulate him in a pleasurable exchange of ideas that would be shared but would ultimately originate in him.

In the biblical fantasy sent to Eduard, different processes are at work (Ibid., p. 28). While the witty references are not always clear, we see that Freud identifies with Jesus and wants to go back to playing cards instead of studying Bacon de Verulam and Descartes. When he responds to Eduard's interest in another friend, he accuses him of trying to become this person's "famulus" even though Roznau is still full of their shared memories. This fit of jealousy is channelled into a moralistic indignation: "You ought to be ashamed of yourself", puzzled by the fact that, in his absence, his friend might stray so far from the path.

5.2.6 Language of the body and sexual identity

Their friendship involves a language of the body already present in Freud's childhood memory of holding onto his father's hand. It is also in relation to his father that he mentions his other favourite sport, swimming. Asking Eduard for a longer letter has to do with what he sees as a lack of expectations, a kind of frugality interpreted as a "fraud". Answering him in a flash is a duty; he wants a "warm friendship" (p. 21) which requires proof.

The plan to go visit Eduard in Roznau collided with Freud's father's designs: "My father does not wish it, and though I long for the place for one hour each day, I cannot seriously plan to do what he for good reasons opposes" (p. 29). In the letter dated 2nd August 1873, this refusal is connected to father's intentions of sending Freud to his uncles in Manchester. At the time, Jacob Freud worried about his son's lack of contact with girls and wanted him to meet Pauline – the little girl in the memory of his childhood games with John. But writing about these memories later, Freud (1899) noted that he could no longer feel the affection he once had for Pauline and did not develop "a new set of fantasies" (Ibid., p. 124). He was a student and completely devoted to his books. "I had nothing left over for my cousin", he wrote, echoing his adult indifference to Gisela. His father and uncle had made a plan for his future: he would give up his abstract studies to choose a more practical subject and, after obtaining his diploma, marry Pauline and set up in Manchester. Freud understood their motives, but given his determination there was nothing more to it. It was only later, as a struggling young scientist, that he could appreciate his father's good intentions in trying "to make good the loss in which the original catastrophe had involved my whole existence", alluding to his early departure from Freiberg (1899, p. 314).

To feel more settled in Vienna and "burn [his] bridges" with his past (Freud, 1871–1881, p. 29), Freud enrolled in a swimming club, without considering that this might pose a problem should he wish to leave town. In his letters, he complains of low water level in the pool, which creates a kind of mud bath where one can neither drown, nor dive, "and with the danger the whole thrill has gone" (Ibid.). In the following letter, he again alludes to his sports activities: while the plan to go to England has been dropped, "contractual, indissoluble ties" bind him to Vienna.

Despite his boredom, he refrains from criticising his father, who is holding him in Vienna, despite being upset at the impossibility of seeing his friend. He alludes to his father's decision by saying that "the main thing, my trip to England, is off", postponed by a year (Ibid., p. 32). Freud's inhibition therefore did not concern only sexuality but also his parricidal wishes – not criticising his father despite the latter's attempts to control his sex life, to decide on whom Freud should meet and where. We see all the elements of the future Oedipus complex coming together, waiting to be theorised.

On starting his medical studies, Freud described the details of his curriculum, which comprised fifty-one and a half hours of weekly lectures, plus his swimming lesson and extra reading. On a postcard from 1876, he writes: "If there were no water or bath in Vienna I should perish from the heat" (Ibid., p. 156).

Swimming was regularly on Freud's mind when he felt down due to a separation – from Eduard, on his trip to Trieste to study eels (Bernfeld, 1951) and later from Martha during their engagement. Sadness, sense of confinement and solitude conjured the image of the pool as a ray of sunshine in his day. As we shall see, the pool also represented the awakening of his post-pubertal sexuality (Freud, 1901). The relationship between his love of swimming and his dreams united the body and its symbolic equivalents, also shown by the role played by arms and hands in his stories.

The tension between the investment and counter-investment of the body was also central to walking and climbing. In the scenes he paints to Eduard, these moments of escape represented a liberation, a sense of freeing oneself internally from the often-suffocating feelings of obligation. On the level of metaphor, such pleasant lightness was accompanied by mental playfulness. Reconnecting with pleasurable physical sensations stimulated a world of less conflictual fantasies revolving around bodily metaphors: the body and its images, such as the heart or the briskly walking legs, the pleasure of eating.

Among these, we notice especially the hands and arms. We remember Freud's disappointment on hearing about his father's lack of heroism in his encounter with the anti-Semite. The hand extended by the father becomes the entanglement of the two friends' arms, the complicity of their at times not quite differentiated duo. This homosexual theme resounds clearly in Freud's repeated demands to revive their Academy, for instance in a letter where he suggests that, according to an old superstition, renewing their secret society requires a double sacrifice. He designates two women, a princess and a queen. Keeping their symbiotic friendship therefore requires the disappearance of girls, who have become an obstacle.

Indeed, their bond was guarded all the more jealously as it helped Freud to keep women at bay, while waiting for the later encounter with Martha. With both Eduard and Martha, and later with Fliess, separation was a true test of patience, a nearly intolerable – that is, quasi-traumatic – ordeal, which in turn required a very tight bond, being as close to the other as possible. Another interpretation might be that a libidinal bond and a painful separation themselves became a way of loving.

The same homosexual current, probably insufficiently elaborated as this would require a decathexis of the paternal figure, later reappeared in Freud's friendship with Fliess. The tone of their correspondence was, at least on Freud's side, very similar, giving their conflict and the eventual breakdown of their relationship its unique colouring. The conflict broke out specifically as a paranoiac crisis around the alleged theft of the idea of psychic bisexuality, an idea that in the friendship with Silberstein had remained latent and can be glimpsed in Freud's dream of the siren (Freud, 1901; Houssier, 2019). Intellectual theft would be one of the sources of tension between Freud and his psychoanalytic "disciples" as well as amongst themselves.

Nevertheless, in the intimate space of Freud's study and his readings, the body is erotically charged through an ascetic abstinence. As a kind of binary opposite, this abstinence contrasts with the bodily images that appear regularly in his writing and of which we find persistent traces in the language of hysteria.

5.2.7 Sigmund and his sisters

Alongside this developing friendship, the two families also met regularly, occasionally providing material for the friends' correspondence. For example, Freud reprimands Eduard for the few lines he sent to his sister Rosa, who allegedly had written him a pages-long letter.

Other comments allude to a parallel conversation between Freud's sisters and Eduard. Freud's requirement of exclusivity was tempered by this "sharing" of Eduard with his sisters, particularly with Anna and Rosa.

Asking whether he is still interested in how his sisters are doing, Freud writes that he is now in charge of Rosa's education, which makes him happy although he has to sacrifice one of his weekly lectures (p. 102). He tells Eduard she has enrolled in a school of drawing and design of feminine handiworks. When Eduard protests, Freud justifies himself by saying that he feels blamed by his friend for his sisters' silence (p. 76), although he has done his best to persuade them to write, specifically during a family council. He also says he has read their letter to Eduard, in which they take an excessively tragic view of some situation – he does not give any details. In the postscript to the letter dated 3rd January 1875, he again asks Eduard why there has been no answer.

Eduard, who in their letters is described as frequently infatuated (Freud, 1873–1939), found his first paramour in Anna Freud, Freud's least favourite sister (contrary to Rosa), and later in Freud's cousin Fanny Philipp, which deepened the feelings of closeness between the two young men and perhaps also, to a smaller degree, Freud's ambivalence vis-à-vis his friend, who was popular with girls, including Freud's sisters. Eduard's success was in stark contrast to Freud's failure with Gisela, which made him subject to intense feelings of loneliness. Let us add that Eduard's interest in Anna revealed to Freud his friend's flirtatious tendencies, what he later called his frivolous levity.

Speaking about his sisters opened another perspective, namely of Freud's dominant role in the family. At the age of twenty, he criticised his sister Rosa, who played the zither and had received some rather flattering praise. He was judgmental about the effect of praise on a young girl's character, telling her she might become vain, coquettish and unbearable. His mother loved music, but despite Freud's youth, he managed to banish the piano from the household. Music ostensibly disrupted him from studying, but more likely he was disturbed by his rivalry with Anna, whom mother wanted to teach how to play. Outside this sibling rivalry he was sensitive to music, which brought out his most deeply buried feelings, defying his need for control when it came to receiving and obtaining pleasure.

We also know that Gisela developed a relationship with the Freud sisters, so that they also gave him an account of her trip to Italy, which greatly affected him. While he behaved authoritatively with his sisters, watching over them as the de facto head of the family, he was distraught by and later rather hostile towards Gisela, who was at first strongly de-idealised in favour of her mother and then seen as an obstacle to fulfilling his professional ambitions.

When speaking to Eduard, Freud's bitter irony towards her barely conceals the teenage boy's disappointment or narcissistic injury; contrary to his sisters, he had no power over Gisela's heart. Throwing himself into his studies was part of his phobic tendencies or, to use Freud's own expression (1916), a way of inventing a diversion. The world of his sisters appeared to replicate the atmosphere of the extended family, from which it was difficult to free oneself, to the point of dreaming about running away (Freud, 1936) to escape the world of the family while indulging one's heroic aspirations.

5.2.8 Matura-tion: the exam and sexual maturity

In July 1873, Freud passed his Matura. It was no accident that for his final essay he chose a subject close to his heart: "Which considerations should guide us in choosing a profession?" He received a distinction. He also had to sit a math exam including problem solving, as well as to translate – already – texts from Latin and Greek into German and also a German text into Latin. His Greek translation, of thirty-three lines from *Oedipus Rex*, earned him the best grade in his class. On the other hand, because he thought the Latin translation was too easy, he did not spend enough time on it and only got a "satisfactory" – an "ignominious failure" in his opinion (Knöpfmacher, 1979). Lastly, he had to pass an oral Latin exam.

He announces to Eduard that he passed his leaving exam with a distinction and brilliant grades: one "excellent", seven "very good" and a commendation in geography. Now that he is free of this burden, he feels lightheaded, as if intoxicated. He wants to be idle, to take his time before telling his friend about this "pitched battle". He promises him a biblical story, but no longer feels the urge to write in a poetic voice (Freud, 1871–1881, p. 19).

Though it was not the only exam he would speak about, the challenge of the *Matura* left a mark in Freud's memory when he was analysing his dreams (1900). The question of becoming a great man or instead missing out on a life of greatness produced an inner tension, which he reveals as a pair of opposites. The analysis of "exam dreams" brings out these reminiscences and points to the masochistic function of these kinds of dreams, which, typically, concern university exams or their substitutes, such as the equivalent of a habilitation defence in Austria at that time. However, they are more frequently mentioned in relation to the *Matura*, which represents a more "typical" dream theme. The anxiety of the situation is interpreted by Freud as a punishment for a child who believes to have misbehaved:

> After we have ceased to be school children, our punishments are no longer inflicted on us by our parents or by those who brought us up or later by our schoolmasters. The relentless causal chains of real life take charge of our further education, and now we dream of Matriculation or Finals (and who has not trembled on those occasions, even if he was well-prepared for the examination?) whenever, having done something wrong or failed to do something properly, we expect to be punished by the event – whenever, in short, we feel the burden of responsibility.
>
> (Ibid., p. 274)

A discussion with a psychoanalyst colleague gave rise to another possible interpretation:

> For a further explanation of examination dreams I have to thank an experienced colleague [Stekel], who once declared at a scientific meeting that so far as he knew dreams of Matriculation only occur in people who have successfully passed it and never in people who have failed in it. It would seem, then, that anxious examination dreams (which, as has been confirmed over and over again, appear when the dreamer has some responsible activity ahead of him next day and is afraid there may be a fiasco) search for some occasion in

the past in which great anxiety has turned out to be unjustified and has been contradicted by the event.

(Ibid.)

It is no surprise that in Freud's dreams, his oedipal ambitions bolstered by adolescence met with their opposite – an instance of failure. He continues:

What is regarded as an indignant protest against the dream: "But I'm a doctor, etc., already!" would in reality be the consolation put forward by the dream, and would accordingly run: "Don't be afraid of tomorrow! Just think how anxious you were before your Matriculation, and yet nothing happened to you. You're a doctor, etc., already."

(Ibid., p. 274)

He was able to verify this hypothesis for himself and for others; he continues to explore his own journey:

For instance, I myself failed in Forensic Medicine in my Finals; but I have never had to cope with this subject in dreams, whereas I have quite often been examined in Botany, Zoology or Chemistry. I went in for the examination in these subjects with well-founded anxiety; but, whether by the grace of destiny or of the examiners, I escaped punishment. In my dreams of school examinations, I am invariably examined in History, in which I did brilliantly – though only, it is true, because [in the oral examination] my kindly master did not fail to notice that on the paper of questions which I handed him back I had run my finger-nail through the middle one of the three questions included, to warn him not to insist upon that particular one.

(Ibid., p. 275)

If accidents are not of particular interest to Freud as an analyst, his tricks during the final exam and the botany exam suggest that these dreams have to do with the teacher in question and his disposition – kindly or otherwise. In the botanical dream, when it comes to testing young Freud's knowledge and given how invested he was in his education, the provisor's harshness represents the intensity of the castration complex. We should remember that Freud sat many exams during his school years, and they provoked much more anxiety than the image of the gifted student, who rarely has to submit to such things, might suggest (Freud, 1925). Even though he was at the top of his class, a failure would have been not just a disappointment to his parents but also make him lose his place as the model child and student, bringing his wish to be the favourite into the school environment.

This libidinal dimension was emphasised when he included examination dreams among the so-called typical dreams, closely linked to his mythical theory of origins (Freud, 1913). Understanding these typical dreams, which humans are said to have had since time immemorial, required collecting a great many examples, which led Freud to write:

> Not long ago, I came to the conclusion that the objection, "You're a doctor, etc., already", does not merely conceal a consolation but also signifies a reproach. This would have run: "You're quite old now, quite far advanced in life, and yet you go on doing these stupid, childish things."
>
> (Freud, 1900, p. 275–276)

This example based on his *Matura* exam uses a memory or event from his teenage years to access the sources of an infantile complex. However, Freud does not close down the debate on the connections between adolescence and infantile sexuality. Like in the case of the screen-memories, his thinking goes on further, towards the enmeshment between infantile and adolescent sexuality. He writes:

> If so, it would not be surprising if the self-reproaches for being "stupid" and "childish" in these last examples referred to the repetition of reprehensible sexual acts. Wilhelm Stekel, who put forward the first interpretation of dreams of Matriculation ["Matura"], was of the opinion that they regularly related to sexual tests and sexual maturity. My experience has often confirmed his view.
>
> (Freud, 1900–1901, p. 276)

This biographical or clinical conclusion suggests that his own post-pubertal sexual maturation was a source of conflict, between the desire for sexual acts and their alleged reprehensibility. As we have seen, this conflict primarily concerned his fantasies of transgressive sexual desires strengthened by the idea of surpassing his father's level of education.

Quite in line with his success in the final exam, the idea of a grand oeuvre that would appeal to Eduard once finished did not leave Freud indifferent. We see it in the comedic megalomania characteristic of his style, when he writes about his numbers system: "you will have to concede that it is a marvellous proof of human perspicacity". And even if "a thousand men cleverer" than himself attend to this theory, his intentions "will be praised, and the eternal glory of the idea will be linked with my name, albeit my successors and those who will stand on my shoulders will outshine me in carrying it out" (Freud, 1871–1881, p. 34). He signs off as the "life member of the famous Spanish Academy, Lord of the Lias and Prince of the Cretaceous", as if the Academy itself has been steeped in his euphoria and grandeur.

Bibliography

Bakan D. (1964), *S. Freud and the Jewish Mystical Tradition*, Paris, Payot.
Bernfeld S. (1922, 1995), Concerning a typical form of male puberty, *Adolescent Psychiatry*, 22, p. 51–66.

Bernfeld S. (1951), Sigmund Freud, M. D., 1882–1885, *International Journal of the Psychoanalysis*, 32, p. 204–217.
Boehlich W. (1990), Introduction, in Freud S. (ed.), *Lettres de jeunesse*, Paris, Gallimard, p. 17–31.
Cervantès M. (1613, 2009), *The Dialogue of the Dogs – The Deceitful Marriage*, Brooklyn, NY, Melville House.
Eissler K. R. (2006), Esquisse biographique, in Eissler K., Freud E., Freud L., Grubitch Simitis I., Fleckhaus W. (dir.), *Sigmund Freud. Lieux, visages, objets*, Paris, Gallimard, p. 10–38.
Freud S. (1871–1881, 1990), *Lettres de jeunesse*, Paris, Gallimard.
Freud S. (1873–1939, 1979), *Correspondance*, Paris, Gallimard.
Freud S. (1898), *Sexuality in the Aetiology of the Neuroses*. SE 3, London, Hogarth Press, p. 259–285.
Freud S. (1899), *Screen Memories*. SE 3, London, Hogarth Press, p. 299–322.
Freud S. (ed.). (1900), *The Interpretation of Dreams*. SE 4, London, Hogarth Press, p. ix–627.
Freud A. (1930, 1969), *Initiation à la psychanalyse pour éducateurs*, Toulouse, Privat.
Freud A. (1936, 1992), *The Ego and the Mechanisms of Defence*, London, Karnac.
Freud S. (1901, 1988), *Sur le rêve*, Paris, Gallimard.
Freud S. (1905), *Three Essays on the Theory of Sexuality*. SE 7, London, Hogarth Press, p. 123–246.
Freud S. (1913), *Totem and Taboo: Some Points of Agreement between the Mental Lives of Savages and Neurotics (1913 [1912–13])*. SE 13, London, Hogarth Press, p. vii–162.
Freud S. (1915, 1986), *Vues d'ensemble sur les névroses de transfert*, Paris, Gallimard.
Freud S. (1916, 1979), *Introduction à la psychanalyse*, Paris, Payot.
Freud S. (1919), *The 'Uncanny'*. SE 17, London, Hogarth Press, p. 217–256.
Freud S. (1925), *An Autobiographical Study*. SE 20, London, Hogarth Press, p. 1–70.
Freud S. (1935), *An Autobiographical Study*. SE 20, London, Hogarth Press, p. 71–74.
Freud S. (1936), *A Disturbance of Memory on the Acropolis*. SE 22, London, Hogarth Press, p. 237–248.
Gallo R. (2009), Freud's Spanish: binlinguism and bisexuality, *Psychoanalysis and History*, 11, p. 5–40.
Gedo J., Wolf E. (1976), Freud's novelas ejemplares, *Psychological Issues*, 34–35, p. 87–111.
Grinberg L., Rodriguez J. F. (1984), The influence of Cervantes on the future creator of the psychoanalysis, *International Journal of Psycho-Analysis*, 65(2), p. 155–168.
Grubrich-Simitis I. (1925, 1984), Introduction, in Freud S. (ed.), *Ma vie et la psychanalyse. Contribution à l'histoire de la psychanalyse*, Paris, Gallimard, p. 7–33.
Hamilton J. W. (2002), Freud and the suicide of Pauline Silberstein, *Psychoanalytic Review*, 89, p. 889–909.
Heim S. (1990), Note liminaire, in S. Freud (ed.), *Lettres de jeunesse*, Paris, Gallimard, p. 7–8.
Houssier F. (2010), *L'école d'Anna Freud. Créativité et controverses*, Paris, Editions Campagne Première.
Houssier F. (2013a), *Meurtres dans la famille*, Paris, Dunod.
Houssier F. (2013b), Sigmund Freud/Eduard Silberstein: une amitié passionnelle et consanguine, *Adolescence*, 83, 31(1), p. 219–226.
Houssier F. (2014), Sauvagerie et confusion: l'adolescence dans le courant post-kleinien, *Topique*, 217, p. 79–93.

Houssier F. (2016), Entre S. Freud et S. Ferenczi, un Œdipe pubertaire?, *Les lettres de la SPF*, 35, p. 157–173.

Houssier F. (2019), *Freud étudiant*, Paris, Campagne-Première.

Knöpfmacher H. (1979), Sigmund Freud in high school, *American Imago*, 36, p. 283–300.

Roudinesco E. (2016), *Freud: In his Time and Ours*, Cambridge, MA, Harvard University Press.

Roudinesco E., Plon M. (1997), *Dictionnaire de la psychanalyse*, Paris, Fayard.

Chapter 6

Conclusions

Having moved between Freud's memories and other passages from his letters documenting his adolescent and student experience, we have now arrived at a waypoint. The moment of passing his school-leaving exam indeed marks a point of maturity that Freud himself considered crucial. As well as confirming Freud's academic talents, it was the source of joy and daydreaming, but also provoked anxiety. Before closing this first page at the end of this rite of passage, let us return to some of the key aspects of his journey.

6.1 This is not a question of age

What can we learn from this first crucial period of Freud's youth? In his family, his role as a first born was all the more prominent given his father's professional shortcomings. When Freud speaks about protecting his sisters alongside his brother Alexander, we understand that this desire was particularly urgent because of his father's inability to provide such protection. Supported by his mother, young Freud therefore acquired a certain degree of power in his family and this further "excited" his incestuous and parricidal fantasies, which resurfaced during his adolescence and populated his dreams. During this time, reading represented not just a way of experiencing his desires through fantasy; its over-investment stemmed from a transgenerational bond (his paternal grandfather, his father and himself) based on a relationship to a religious text, the Torah. His asceticism emerged at the intersection of this epistemophilic mandate and oedipal desire, namely as a wish to develop new knowledge and thus become a great man. His sexual inhibitions were reinforced by this "mission", which naturally generated certain megalomaniac fantasies, reflected in his attraction to the work of Cervantes.

His strongly ascetic leaning was matched by his revolutionary tendencies. These were already present in the episode in which Freud, aged just seven or eight, disobeyed his father by urinating in his parents' room and was punished for it. His revolt carried the traces of oedipal (and no doubt preoedipal) conflict in his relationships to paternal figures, which would persist in his friendships throughout his life. The image of his revolt turned out to be very productive, because it entailed a "successful" displacement. Like the monk Philammon tormented by

DOI: 10.4324/9781003340898-6

his desires for his sister, Freud withdrew into the world of ideas, which became a refuge for his libido. A confrontation with his father in order to surpass him required an ideological revolt, a wish to surpass the intellectual leaders of his time by creating a new theory – a fantasy of a deadly intellectual revolution. In the next volume of this work, which focuses on Freud's life as a student and a young scientist (Houssier, 2019), we shall see this revolutionary search for ideas, constantly repeated throughout Freud's life, being pushed further. Later in his life, on the political and social level, his wish to prevent neurosis in as many people as possible or his plea for premarital sexual liberty attest to the creativity inspired by this nodal point of inner conflict. Reading these letters, full of turmoil and teenage conflict, opens up new configurations.

While Breger focuses on the challenges of loss in Freud's early attachments to his mother and nursemaid, his romantic passion for mother-daughter couples, which we see emerge in these letters, suggests that in terms of erotic investment, young Freud more spontaneously made the association with the figures of mother and sister. In any case, in addition to his pursuit of a friendship with Eduard as a form of a double, there was also an other who was doubly eroticised. We can also glimpse his rivalry with his sister Anna; however, he would later intervene to prevent her marriage to a man he deemed too old for her, just like he did in the case of Ernest Jones, whose behaviour towards his daughter Anna he considered overly seductive. While it is often said that Rosa was Sigmund's favourite sister, it would seem that his connection with Anna was more intensely invested. Perhaps its ambivalence also reappeared in his relationship to Gisela Fluss?

A first tipping point between the two periods of his adolescence can be located by connecting the two central figures of his youth, Eduard and Martha. We have seen Freud's penchant for book burning, when already as a young boy he suggested to Eduard that they burn some of their "works" together. As a young man engaged to Martha Bernays, Freud assured his fiancée he would do no such thing with her letters; by keeping his promise, he gave us access to a later period of his youth, the first four years of their courtship. We can of course question whether this correspondence, now considered a gem of amorous literature, can really be thought of as the writing of an adolescent. However, in their analysis of these letters, Grubitch-Simitis and Lortholary (2012), authors little known for their interest in adolescence, conclude that the positions taken by Freud in his letters to his fiancée remain precisely of this nature. This leads me to argue, as Freud did regarding Jung (1914), that the youthfulness of a person does not depend on their age, suggesting we understand adolescence as a process rather than a specific age bracket. This idea, put forth by Freud in his critique of Jung, also resonates with his diagnosis of Ferenczi's "third puberty". I will not return here to Freud's own ambivalence regarding his teenage years; it suffices to say that this emergent thought in his comment on Jung suggests a "subliminal" theorisation of adolescence, as a negative object of Freud's thought. The remark regarding Jung clashes with his own argument that the transformations of puberty had well-defined limits, from the onset of puberty to the end of adolescence (Freud, 1905). It also echoes a somewhat provocative question raised by Philippe Gutton: "But why do we want adolescence to end?" I think this question tries to separate the process of adolescence from all types of normative developmental theorisations. It argues that adolescence cannot be reduced to a question of age or psycho-social factors (entering the sphere of work, leaving the parental home) and instead opens up the following perspective: while puberty is indeed the biological bedrock of adolescence, the latter's ending remains suspended when we think of it as of elaborating one's own position while also undergoing change (Marty, 2009). The process of profound transformation that begins at adolescence would then not result in a specific outcome but rather would be elaborated following an inner rhythm, where its traces would remain alive in each individual, beyond any normative criteria. Emotionally and intrapsychically, the infantile and adolescence both leave an indelible mark on a subject's history, such as for example in every person's relationship to culture, where the drive for knowledge combines with the key discoveries, in our youth, of our individual cultural passions. As we have seen, this investment of cultural objects as a point of articulation between the infantile and the adolescent is particularly prominent in Freud's case.

6.2 An adolescence avoided

In this perspective, Freud's life journey offers us a paradigmatic example of modern adolescence. While the question remains open, we can at least assume that it was a rather long journey, if we see the importance of a love relationship as a sign of having made the shift from the primary love-object to a non-incestuous object. Remember that he only met his future wife, Martha Bernays, when he was twenty-six. Between his infatuation with Gisela and this new encounter, we do not know of any other romantic interests. However, we can presume that during these ten years of emotional solitude and imaginary life his capacities of elaboration were greatly relied on and even prepared him for a genuine encounter with an object. This psychical availability as well as the pain of waiting are very obvious in his letters to his fiancée. Already as a teenager, Freud spoke about his sadness and connected it to the fact that his friends, such as Emil or Eduard, were experiencing what he himself was only reading and dreaming about. Later, many examples point to his depressive moods: "To be healthy is so wonderful if one isn't condemned to be alone" (Freud, 1873–1939, p. 142), he wrote to his fiancée, though he himself often suffered from ill health due to his neurasthenia. The fact that he experienced his solitude as a condemnation suggests that despite masking his interest in girls by his emphasis on study, this absence still weighed on him. Looking back, depressive and negative feelings made his sense of unhappiness prior to meeting his fiancée seem extremely acute, contrary to the manic and slightly megalomaniac positions we find in his letters to Eduard. Let's look at a few striking examples (Ibid., p. 202): "In my youth I was never young", which we could link to the subsequent "I have always restrained myself" (p. 203). "Before meeting you, I felt completely indifferent to life" (Ibid.), he also wrote, giving us a glimpse of the deep sense of despair, which he illustrates also as follows: "If I hadn't found you [. . .] I would just have strayed miserably about and gone into a decline" (p. 57). The exaltation of his love for Martha is thus also due to her being his saviour. No need to add more to show that despite his academic and professional achievement, Freud's adolescence, between his feelings of solitude and abstinence, was indeed painful. A detail echoing the language shared with Eduard, regarding the "principles", nevertheless deserves a mention:

> Before I met you, I didn't know the joy of living, and now that "in principle" you are mine, to have you completely is the one condition I make to life, which I otherwise don't set any great story by.
>
> (p. 113)

Freud's candour towards Martha is both touching and revealing. We can see the consequences of his infantile-adolescent conflicts when in a letter to her from January 1886 (Ibid.) he complains that he lacks the "indefinite something which attracts people" and this has deprived him of "a rosy existence". He adds poverty, the success that was so slow to come, his hyper-sensibility and nervousness into the mix:

> I believe people see something alien in me and the real reason for this is that in my youth I was never young and now that I am entering the age of maturity I cannot mature properly. There was a time when I was all ambition and eager to learn, when day after day I felt aggrieved that nature had not, in one of her benevolent moods, stamped my face with that mark of genius which now and again she bestows on men.
>
> (p. 202)

The last remark is not without importance. The phobic escape from relationships with "principles" pushed Freud towards intellectualisation. Missing out on one's youth implies an adolescence sacrificed on the altar of the drive for knowledge. After first having rejected love and then desperately waiting for it to come, Freud's encounter with Martha provoked an acute sense of nostalgia that kept him stuck. To have neither youth nor the desire to achieve true maturity meant that the wish to remain young became one of his recurrent desires, which appeared regularly in his dreams. Lastly, the fact that his youth had been different than that of his peers and could not be relived points out to the aspects of his adolescence that remained insufficiently elaborated.

The decisive and transformative encounter with Martha was preceded by Freud's life as a student and his first professional steps, two critical periods during which he was searching for figures of identifications that were essentially paternal. Over time, Freud learnt to take a position and became able to defend himself against bullying and overt anti-Semitism. On becoming a young man, we see another face of him: more assertive about his desires and ready to expunge his father's humiliation. From one epistolary relationship to another, his letters to Martha, now considered a prime example of 19th-century love literature, are essential to understanding his experience during this phase of his life.

We can thus ultimately conclude by inviting the reader to visit these new regions of *terra freudiana*: To be continued . . .

Bibliography

Breger L. (2000), *Freud: Darkness in the Midst of Vision*, New York, Wiley.

Cervantès M. (1613, 2009), *The Dialogue of the Dogs – The Deceitful Marriage*, Brooklyn, NY, Melville House.

Freud S. (1905), *Three Essays on the Theory of Sexuality*. SE 7, London, Hogarth Press, p. 123–246.

Freud S. (1914), *On the History of the Psycho-Analytic Movement*. SE 14, London, Hogarth Press, p. 1–66.

Freud S. (1979), *Correspondance (1873–1939)*, Paris, Gallimard.

Grubitch-Simitis I., Lortholary B. (2012), L'affectif et la théorie Sigmund et Martha: prélude freudien Germes de concepts psychanalytiques fondamentaux. À propos des lettres de fiancés de Sigmund Freud et Martha Bernays, *Revue Française de Psychanalyse*, 3(76), p. 779–795.

Gutton P. (1996), *Le pubertaire*, Paris, PUF.

Gutton P. (2004), Une création à l'Université: l'unité de recherches Adolescence, *Recherches en psychanalyse*, 1, p. 21–26.

Houssier F. (2019), *Freud étudiant*, Paris, Campagne-Première.

Marty F. (2009), Quand le fantasme prend corps, in J. André (sous la dir.), *La psychanalyse de l'adolescence existe-t-elle?*, Paris, PUF, p. 205–222.

Index

For Product Safety Concerns and Information please contact our EU
representative GPSR@taylorandfrancis.com
Taylor & Francis Verlag GmbH, Kaufingerstraße 24, 80331 München, Germany

www.ingramcontent.com/pod-product-compliance
Lightning Source LLC
Chambersburg PA
CBHW050616280326
41932CB00016B/3070